The Spiritual Life
of
CARDINAL MERRY DEL VAL

Cardinal Rafael Merry del Val

The Spiritual Life
of
CARDINAL MERRY DEL VAL

By
REV. JEROME DAL-GAL

Translated by
REV. JOSEPH A. McMULLIN, PH.D., D.D.

Originally published by:

BENZIGER BROTHERS, Inc.

Reprinted exactly from the original
by

Mediatrix Press
MMXIV

ISBN: 0692337776
©Mediatrix Press 2014.

This Work is in the pubic domain.

Nihil Obstat:
                    JOSEPH A. M. QUIGLEY
                        Censor Librorum

Imprimatur:
               ✠ JOHN CARDINAL O'HARA, C.S.C.
                 Archiepiscopus Philadelphiensis
                  Philadelphiae, 22 Januarii 1959

The nihil obstat and imprimatur are official declarations that a book or pamphlet is free of doctrinal or moral error. No implication is contained therein that those who have granted the nihil obstat and imprimatur agree with the contents, opinions, or statements expressed.

Table of Contents

I	*From Sunrise to Noon(1865-1930)*..........	-5-
II	*The Secretary of State*....................	-27-
III	*Portrait of a Man*........................	-55-
IV	*Apostle in Rome*.........................	-69-
V	*Prayer and Penance*......................	-83-
VI	*Union with God*..........................	-97-
VII	*The Director of Souls*....................	-113-
VIII	*Hidden with Christ*......................	-127-
IX	*In the Footsteps of the Saints*.............	-145-
	Epilogue..	-169-

"The glory of mankind is enriched by the splendor of virtue"
-ST. AUGUSTINE

Chronology

1865—His Birth in London.

1875—His First Holy Communion.

1876—At the College of Our Lady of Peace in Namur. 1878—At St. Michael's College in Brussels.

1883—At the Seminary of St. Cuthbert, Ushaw, England.

1885—Received Minor Orders.

1885—Student at the Accademia dei Nobili Ecclesiastici in Rome.

1887—Appointed Honorary Private Chamberlain with the title of Monsignor by Pope Leo XIII and sent to London as Secretary to Monsignor Ruffo Scilla to offer congratulations to Queen Victoria on her Golden Jubilee.

1887—Received the Subdiaconate at Prague.

1888—Named Secretary of the Special Papal Mission to Berlin for the funeral of Emperor William I and the coronation of Emperor Frederick III.

1888—Ordained Deacon and Priest at Rome by His Eminence Cardinal Lucido Maria Parocchi, Vicar-General of His Holiness.

1889—Named Secretary of the Special Papal Mission to the Imperial Court of Vienna.

1891—Appointed a Papal Chamberlain on active duty with His Holiness.

1893—Named Apostolic Delegate to Hungary to present the Red Hat to the new Cardinal, Lawrence Schlauch, Bishop of Gran Varadino.

1895—Named Associate Secretary of the Special Papal Commission for the Union of Dissident Churches.

1896—Named Secretary of the Special Commission of Cardinals for the study of the validity of Anglican Orders.

1897—Appointed Domestic Prelate by His Holiness and Special Apostolic Delegate to Canada.

1898—Named a Consultor of the Sacred Congregation of the Index.

1899—Chosen President of the Pontificia Accademia dei Nobili Ecclesiastici.

1900—Named titular Archbishop of Nicaea.

1902—Sent as Special Envoy to London for the Coronation of King

Edward VII.

1903—Named Secretary of the Sacred College and Secretary of the Conclave in the election of St. Pius X.

1903—Appointed Pro-Secretary of State.

1903—Appointed Secretary of State and a Cardinal of the Holy Roman Church.

1913—Celebrated His Silver Jubilee in the Priesthood.

1914—Named Archpriest of the Vatican Basilica.

1914—Appointed Secretary of the Sacred Congregation of the Holy Office.

1920—Sent as Papal Legate to Assisi for the first Centenary of the finding of the body of St. Francis of Assisi.

1925—Celebrated His Silver Jubilee as a Bishop.

1926—Sent as Papal Legate to Assisi for the seventh Centenary of the death of St. Francis of Assisi.

1928—Celebrated His Silver Jubilee as a Cardinal.

1930—His holy death in Vatican City.

"The Cardinal Secretary of State of St. Pius X belongs, like his Sovereign, to history; but, as a Priest, he belongs to the Church which he adorned and embellished with the splendor of his piety: he belongs to the pious devotion of those souls who understood and appreciated the austerity and mortification of his life: he belongs to the infinite number of people he comforted and helped with spiritual guidance and material assistance in time of trouble and need."
        Osservatore Romano—February 25, 1932

From Sunrise to Noon

(1865-1930)

"How different my life has been from what I had hoped for! God's will be done!"
CARDINAL MERRY DEL VAL

I

From Sunrise to Noon
(1865-1930)

St. Pius X had as his Secretary of State a man who was eminently worthy of his holy pontificate—Cardinal Merry del Val. In 1931, a year after the death of this illustrious Cardinal, the famous French scholar Rene Bazin made the following observation:

"Judgment was passed in many different ways on Cardinal Merry del Val while he was living. This was due largely to the part he played in the political and religious affairs of his time. But now that he is dead people are getting to know him better, for with death has come the unveiling of the well-guarded secret of his extraordinary spiritual life."

Many people have admired the Cardinal for the role he played in one of the most difficult and turbulent pontificates the Church has ever seen. Comparatively few, however, have been able to see beyond his successful career and penetrate into that deep interior life which gave his earthly existence a definitely supernatural imprint. It is this spiritual side of the Cardinal's life that we intend to stress. We shall rely upon evidence drawn not only from the events of his life and the many phases of his work, but also—and particularly—from the austere beauty of his silent virtues, from the holiness of his teaching, and from the lasting impression this servant of God made upon the entire world.

It seems essential to see the figure of priest, bishop, and Cardinal against this background simply because his great priestly virtues, concealed under the appearance of an

The Spiritual Life of Cardinal Merry del Val

ordinary life, should be made known in order to become a source of inspiration for so many who remain unaware of them. His virtues are all the more remarkable when one considers that he lived amid the splendor of two papal courts and was burdened all the while with grave responsibilities in the handling of the difficult affairs of the Church.

The future Secretary of State of St. Pius X was the second child born to Marquis Raphael Merry del Val—a distinguished diplomat of ancient Spanish and Irish lineage—and Countess Josephine de Zulueta of a prominent English family tracing its origins back to Spain. Young Raphael first saw the light of day on October 10, 1865, in London where his father was Secretary to the Spanish Embassy. The child was baptized a day later by Canon H. Hearn in the chapel of the embassy.

Since his ancestors were of different nationalities, there flowed through his veins the blood of some of the most famous families of Ireland, England, Spain, Scotland, and Holland, and with it he inherited some of their best characteristics and finest qualities. By his life he added luster to a noble family already renowned for its stanch loyalty to the Church. Among his forebears was a martyr of the Church, St. Dominguito del Val, a child barely seven years old when crucified to a wall in the cathedral of Saragossa in 1250 by the enemies of Christianity.

One could almost say that Raphael was born with the desire to be a priest. When he was just eight years old, one day in 1873 his mother took him to visit her uncle, Father Francis de Zulueta of the Society of Jesus. An elderly Jesuit Father asked the child what he wanted to be when he grew up. Without the slightest hesitation, he replied: "I want to be a priest!"

In the evening his nurse used to take him in to say good

From Sunrise to Noon

night to his parents. Once he pulled a little wafer out of the sleeve of his suit and, lifting it up, said with childlike simplicity: "This is what I shall do with the Host when I become a priest." Another time he was sitting at the dining table in the home of his maternal grandmother. Suddenly he picked up a glass of water and a wafer, lifted them slightly, and said: "This is what I shall do when I say Mass."

Nature had given Raphael a lively disposition and he enjoyed setting up little altars and imitating the ceremonies of the Holy Sacrifice. He liked to be near the priests that visited his parents and often told them all about his miniature altars, about his "Masses," or about the prayers he had learned by heart. At times he put questions to them that revealed an intelligence and intuition far beyond his years and at the same time showed that he already had some awareness of a divine call.

Raphael's pious mother started his training by instilling in him a deep and practical sense of Christian living; then he began his elementary education in the preparatory school of Bayliss House at Slough. In keeping with the strict educational system of those days, he soon learned to mold his spirit with that strength of character and will power which later on would prove to be the secret of his brilliant achievements. It was here that he was to receive the Sacrament of Confirmation.

In 1875, when he was ten years of age, he first received Our Lord in the Blessed Sacrament. All those present at his First Holy Communion, which took place in the church of the Jesuit Fathers at Bournemouth, were edified by his piety and fervor.

Raphael completed his classical studies under the tutelage of the Jesuits, first in the College of Our Lady of Peace at Namur (1876-77), and then in St. Michael's College (now St. John Berchmans') at Brussels (1878- 83). His keenness of

The Spiritual Life of Cardinal Merry del Val

intellect and application to duty made him outstanding, but it was his singular piety that endeared him to all.

Every year Raphael came out first in all his subjects and was praised highly for his work, and it was usual to see after his name some such annotation as "Very Good" or "Highest number of credits." Teachers, professors, and classmates all held him in high esteem for his high ideals and unfailing joviality, and for his sincere and open character. They all predicted big things for him; everybody agreed that "He would turn out to be a most extraordinary man." Future events proved just how right they were.

But no one suspected that a priest of God was being formed in young Merry del Val. He loved to play tennis and cricket, not to mention chess. He was an outstanding horseman and fencer. In fact, he lent himself with surprising ability to any sort of sports, not only to round out an education demanded by the high social standing of his family, but also to strengthen his rather delicate constitution that from time to time was a source of worry to his parents.

Through quiet study and devout prayer, and under the watchful care of expert teachers, Raphael's priestly vocation began gradually to assume definite proportions. It could be seen in the innocence and tranquillity of his eyes, in the modest reserve of his speech, in his dignified and distinguished bearing. It showed particularly, however, in the instinctive distaste he experienced every time his duties called him to mingle with high society or when someone suggested that he could have a brilliant military career.

By now Raphael had made up his mind what he wanted to do; he had decided to follow the voice of the Divine Master calling him to the priesthood. Deep down in his heart he cherished the hope that he might be able to dedicate himself to the conversion of his native land, a country he loved so much, particularly in view of the tragic

From Sunrise to Noon

circumstances which had separated it from the unity of the Church of Christ.

The outstanding characteristic of his priestly vocation, the bright light that difficult tasks and heavy responsibilities would never succeed in obscuring, was summed up in the words which he wanted to have written on his tomb: "Give me souls; take away all else."

In 1883, at the age of eighteen, in the flower of youth with all its promise and allurements, the son of Ambassador Merry del Val decided to forgo the opportunities of a life in the world. Heeding the voice of God, he entered St. Cuthbert's Seminary at Ushaw[1] to begin the studies that would prepare him for the priesthood and train him so that he could one day step out into the fields ripe for harvest and work for the conversion of his Anglican brethren.

To test the strength of his resolution, his father called him in one day and said: "How will you ever manage to be a priest, Raphael, with your great love for sports, games, and riding?" Without the slightest bit of hesitation his son replied: "We can and we ought to sacrifice everything for God."

Young Raphael Merry del Val completed his course in philosophy and received Minor Orders. Cardinal Vaughan, then Archbishop of Westminster, had come to like him very much, and in the fall of 1885 expressed the desire that he go to Rome. Together with his father, Spanish Ambassador at that time to the imperial court of Vienna, he arrived in Rome to begin his theological studies at the Scots College.

When Pope Leo XIII heard that the Spanish Ambassador was in Rome, he wanted to receive him and his son

---

[1] The famous University of Ushaw dating back to 1794 is today the regional seminary of the province of Liverpool and the diocese of Shrewsbury.

The Spiritual Life of Cardinal Merry del Val

immediately at a private audience. The venerable Pontiff, a keen student of human nature, was greatly impressed with the aristocratic appearance of the youthful cleric. The Pope graciously inquired all about the young man's studies, his vocation, and his plans for the future, all the while carefully observing him and weighing his answers.

"Now where is it you said this young man is going?" asked the Pope, turning to his father.

"He is entering the Scots College, Your Holiness."

"Why the Scots College?" asked the Pope. Then, after a brief pause, he added in the tone of one issuing an order: "Not the Scots College, but the Accademia dei Nobili Ecclesiastici"—the college for the training of priests in the Church's diplomatic service.

In compliance with the express wish of the Holy Father, two days later Ambassador Merry del Val's son entered the Accademia. He was the only unordained student there, and certainly one of the youngest.

In order better to attain the sanctity and perfection he so ardently desired, young Merry del Val made it a point to forgo small liberties that were permitted by the rules of the institution. He restricted himself voluntarily to a much more severe mode of living and divided his time between study and prayer, stimulated by the thought of becoming a priest and dedicating himself to the salvation of souls.

In the fall he spent his vacation with his family at Vienna where his father continued as Spanish Ambassador. There he came into contact with the aristocracy, even with the imperial court itself. Wherever he went, people admired him; his manners were so distinguished, his entire bearing so definitely noble, his looks so strikingly handsome. But, apart from visits and receptions that were always a bit of a burden to him, he kept to himself and led a life of recollection.

From Sunrise to Noon

Young Merry del Val's excellent education and background, his perfect mastery of the principal European languages, the diplomatic traditions of his family—all this inevitably recommended him to the Holy Father. When only twenty-two years old and not yet a priest, in June of 1887, Leo XIII appointed him a Supernumerary Private Chamberlain. With this honorary post there goes, of course, the title of Monsignor. Thus, something really unique in our day, young Merry del Val was a Monsignor while still a student and not yet ordained. This in itself is sufficient proof of how highly Leo XIII regarded him. The Pope also sent him to London with Monsignor Ruffo Scilla, as Secretary of the Papal Mission which was to offer congratulations to Queen Victoria on her golden jubilee.

After his return from London, the young Monsignor went right back to his customary life of study and recollection in preparation for the subdiaconate. He was ordained subdeacon on September 29th of that same year in the cathedral of Prague by His Eminence Cardinal Schönborn, Archbishop of Prague and an intimate friend of Ambassador Merry del Val.

Leo XIII, however, kept his eye on Raphael, and in March, 1888, showed once more how much regard and confidence he had in him. He was appointed Secretary of the Papal Mission which, under Monsignor Galimberti, Apostolic Nuncio to Austria, was to represent the Holy Father in Berlin at the funeral of Emperor William I and at the subsequent coronation of the new Emperor, Frederick III.

Thus the venerable Pontiff made good use of Monsignor Merry del Val's many exceptional talents which lent greater dignity to Papal Missions in various courts of Europe, which the Pope, a born ruler himself, always held in such high regard.

These honorary papal assignments served in no way,

The Spiritual Life of Cardinal Merry del Val

however, to distract the young student of the Accademia from his piety and recollection, for all he could ever see on his everyday horizon was his one and only goal: God! The only deep emotion that stirred within his heart was the salvation of souls! He longed for that solemn hour when he would scale the heights of the priesthood.

That hour was now not too far off. On March 27, 1888, the Feast of the Most Blessed Trinity, he was ordained deacon by His Eminence Cardinal Lucido Maria Parocchi, Vicar General of His Holiness, and on December 30 of that same year he was ordained a priest. What a revelation it would have been for His Eminence Cardinal Parocchi if someone were to have told him that in the young Levite he had just ordained the Lord was preparing a Secretary of State for that future Pope whom just four years before the Cardinal had consecrated Bishop of Mantua.

Two days later, on January 1, 1889, with deep humility Monsignor Merry del Val celebrated his First Mass in the "Rooms of St. Ignatius" just off the beautiful Church of the Gesù in Rome. His parents and intimate friends were the only ones present.

Now he could devote himself completely to the care of souls. His lips which had uttered the words of command to God Himself could now speak divine words of absolution; his hands, still sweet-smelling from the holy chrism, could be joined more ardently than ever in prayer and extended over others in the act of blessing. He was completely unaware, however, of the lofty plans God had arranged for him in His providence just as, a few years before, he had had no idea that the St. Cuthbert's Seminary was to lead him to the threshold of Rome.

Another honorary assignment awaited Monsignor Merry del Val as soon as he was ordained a priest. In December of 1889 Leo XIII sent him to Vienna on a special Papal Mission

From Sunrise to Noon

to present a gift from His Holiness to His Majesty Francis Joseph, Emperor of Austria and Hungary.

Monsignor Merry del Val paid little heed to the glory of such earthly honors—a bit of dust to be swept away by the wind—and thoughts of a far more sublime nature formed the object of his daily meditations, the dedication of himself to the salvation of souls. Without any further delay, therefore, although he had not yet completed his studies at the Gregorian University nor the special course in ecclesiastical diplomacy at the Accademia, he began exercising his ministry whenever he could find a bit of free time. He worked among the children in the thickly populated section of Trastevere, in various churches and religious institutions of Rome, and among those English-speaking groups of higher society either living in Rome or just passing through the Eternal City. He possessed the energy and zeal of a true apostle, and love for Christ burned brightly within him: "Give me souls; take away all else" was then as always the dominant passion of his life.

The future Secretary of State for a saintly Pope thus carried out a program of highly successful apostolic work and became known as a priest of singular piety as well as a gentleman of solid and extraordinary culture. Then on December 31, 1891, Leo XIII called him to the Vatican and appointed him Papal Chamberlain on active duty. To young Monsignor Merry del Val it seemed almost as if an insurmountable obstacle had been put in his way that would certainly prevent him from realizing the goal of his dreams, to dedicate his life to the conversion of "our separated brethren" in his beloved England.

With deep humility he made known to the Holy Father just what it was that bothered him and also what he most wanted to do. He begged that he be left alone in the vocation of a simple priest. The Holy Father answered him with this

The Spiritual Life of Cardinal Merry del Val

question:

"Tell me, Monsignor, are you fully prepared to obey the Pope and to serve the Church?"

Monsignor Merry del Val was deeply moved by the Pontiff's display of confidence in him and murmured in reply: "Yes, whatever Your Holiness commands."

"Very well," concluded the Pontiff, and that ended the interview.

The young Monsignor bowed to the will of the Holy Father and without turning back or looking ahead, but with the firm resolution of a man taking upon his shoulders a burden of honor, he threw himself wholeheartedly into the new life the Lord had mapped out for him. It was a life he himself had never expected or dreamed of, but the course of his life had thus been set, for God was now getting him ready to be one day a brilliant light of the Church.

Leo XIII possessed that rather uncommon faculty of being able to surround himself with capable men. He wanted young Monsignor Merry del Val near him, knowing that he could make good use of him in any religious matters that might come up with respect to English-speaking countries, particularly England which had always been an object of utmost concern to the Holy Father. The Monsignor exhibited a scrupulous sense of responsibility in carrying out the wishes of the venerable Pontiff.

How well Monsignor Merry del Val worked, sometimes with great personal sacrifice, for the welfare of the Church in England is attested by the correspondence he carried on from 1895 to 1903 with Monsignor Rinaldo Angeli, the Private Secretary of Leo XIII. On every page and in every line you can see the reflection of his personal holiness, of his humble feelings in the matter, and of the wisdom of his viewpoints.

From Sunrise to Noon

Another fact to be kept in mind is the way Cardinal Vaughan, Archbishop of Westminster, placed such implicit and complete confidence in him. Actually, Cardinal Vaughan hesitated to take any important action without first asking the Monsignor's opinion or seeking his advice. His Eminence considered him to be the most trustworthy and reliable spokesman in Rome for the Church in England.

Monsignor Merry del Val's perfect application to duty is shown by the actual amount of work he personally put into the Pope's encyclical of April 14, 1895, in which the Holy Father made an ardent appeal for a unity of minds and hearts in the one true Faith. It was really this work which merited for him the following December promotion to Associate Secretary of the Special Papal Commission for the Union of Dissident Oriental Churches.

As Secretary of the Special Commission of Cardinals set up to investigate the important matter of Anglican Orders, Monsignor Merry del Val furnished additional proof of his zeal. His thorough study and research were to serve as an outline for the basic ideas incorporated in the famous encyclical *Apostolicae curae* of September 13, 1896, in which the Holy Father made a definite pronouncement on the invalidity of Anglican Orders. Uncertainty in this matter had been a serious obstacle preventing many well-intentioned but misguided minds from returning to the unity of the Church of Rome. The value of Monsignor Merry del Val's work in the important matter of Anglican Orders becomes perfectly obvious to anyone reading the dissertation he published in the *Civiltà Cattolica* under the title: "Apropos of Anglican Orders: an Unpublished Document." This article stirred up much interest in the press, both Catholic and Protestant, and won him a reputation as an eminent theologian as well as a gifted controversial writer.

To appreciate the importance of these studies we must

The Spiritual Life of Cardinal Merry del Val

keep in mind that toward the end of the nineteenth century fresh impetus had been given the controversy concerning the validity of Sacred Orders conferred according to the Anglican rite introduced by Edward VI. The Anglican hierarchy naturally held for their validity. This opinion was also maintained by some Catholic writers who thought that such a stand would make it easier for the Anglicans to return to the true Church of Christ. Leo XIII was deeply concerned with the matter and after a prolonged and deep study of the complex problem declared that Orders conferred according to the rite of Edward VI were invalid.

A well-known and learned Roman prelate, Monsignor Ruffini, later made the following observation apropos of Leo XIII's declaration: "The salutary effects of this declaration were and still are too numerous to be counted. It is no exaggeration to say it marked the beginning of that deviation from Anglicanism which started with the son of the Anglican Archbishop of Canterbury, Robert Hugh Benson, who became a Catholic and then a priest. It has continued to the present day and has brought an immense multitude of erring souls into the kingdom of truth."

The Pope was highly pleased with the untiring work of Monsignor Merry del Val and, to show his gratitude, in March of 1897 appointed him a Domestic Prelate and the Special Apostolic Delegate to Canada. The bilingual factions in Manitoba—French and English—were hotly engaged at that time in a discussion of a political and religious nature. Because of the discord then sweeping through Canada, the settlement of this controversy required the utmost prudence and a fine diplomatic touch.

Civil authorities in Manitoba had promulgated certain laws on education that were at variance with family rights and the freedom of the Church. These laws were interpreted

From Sunrise to Noon

in various ways, even by Catholics, the diversity of opinions being due in part to political and nationalistic attitudes. Consequently, Leo XIII sent Monsignor Merry del Val to Canada in order to get some clear-cut information on this vital and perplexing problem.

The Pope's choice of a comparatively unknown prelate, only thirty-two years old, for a mission so far away and in such a delicate matter naturally caused considerable consternation and no little comment. It was an assignment that would require detailed investigation and numerous contacts with archbishops and bishops, with ministers of state and governors, with senators and deputies often of opposite parties and conflicting ideas. But the Holy Father knew what he was doing; he was well aware of the youthful Apostolic Delegate's great ability and exceptional talent.

Monsignor Merry del Val remained in Canada for three months, from April 1 to July 3, 1897. We have the word of the Holy Father himself as to just how well he accomplished his mission.

In approbation of the work done by Monsignor Merry del Val, the Pope wrote an encyclical letter to the Canadian hierarchy on December 8, 1897, in which he made a formal declaration that his Apostolic Delegate carried out his mandate "diligently and faithfully." In view of this splendid testimonial of Leo XIII it is certainly not surprising that Monsignor Merry del Val left behind him in Canada a lasting impression and unforgettable memories.

Cardinal Luigi Sincero, Secretary of the Sacred Congregation for the Oriental Church, returning from Canada thirty-one years later, wrote to Cardinal Merry del Val: "I have a pleasant duty to perform; I want to extend to Your Eminence heartfelt greetings from all those in Canada, especially from prominent members of the laity who were fortunate enough to meet you. The Governor and the Chief

The Spiritual Life of Cardinal Merry del Val

Justice of Quebec still remember with a deep sense of gratitude the visit Your Eminence paid to Canada, for they look upon it as the beginning of and the reason behind the peace and harmony that now prevails."

Monsignor Merry del Val left the Vatican in October, 1899, to assume his new post as President of the Accademia dei Nobili Ecclesiastici where just eight years before he had been enrolled as a student. Then, a short while later the Holy Father conferred upon him the fullness of the priesthood by appointing him Titular Archbishop of Nicaea on April 19, 1900.

The young Archbishop scrupulously observed the rules of the Academy and made it his practice to attend all the exercises of the community. He was the first in chapel in the morning and would read the points of meditation. He never absented himself from the refectory at meal times, and after both dinner and supper he would take his recreation together with the students. He liked to engage them in pleasant and uplifting conversation. In the event anyone became sick or suffered a bereavement at home, he was always on hand to offer solace and comfort. He was never forced to take any strong disciplinary measures; just a word, a gesture, or a look from him was all that was ever necessary.

The most important thing to Archbishop Merry del Val was training the young men entrusted to him in the spirit of priestly holiness so that they might be able to serve the Church and the Holy Father with true love and loyalty. As a result, he never left the Academy unless his office demanded it or his priestly duties required it of him. Whenever he did go out, he made it a point to be back before the ringing of the Ave Maria bell. Bishop de Raymond, who was well acquainted with him during this

From Sunrise to Noon

time, writes:

"He lived entirely for his work and was never seen at receptions given by high society unless there was some definite good to be accomplished by his presence there. The Holy Father, who was extremely fond of him, would ask him at times to be present at affairs given by his father, at that time Ambassador of Spain to the Holy See, and he would go out of obedience. But it was easy to see by his whole attitude that he did not like to be there. He felt and acted like a fish out of water."

The example of the young Archbishop was in itself an unspoken sermon, a constant source of edification, and a daily incentive to do one's duty and strive toward perfection and holiness.

After a quarter of a century spent in enriching Holy Mother Church with his wisdom and knowledge and sagely directing her course, on July 20, 1903, the illustrious Pontiff of the Social Question closed his eyes in death. All over the world Catholics offered up prayers for the Church and for the deceased Leo XIII. While the people of Rome bowed their heads in sorrow be fore the mortal remains of the venerable ninety-year old Pope, princes of the Church from all over the world started toward Rome for the conclave that would give the Church a new shepherd and Christ a new vicar.

A few days before the death of Leo XIII, Monsignor Volpini, Secretary of the Consistorial Congregation, had suddenly collapsed in the antechamber of the Pope and died a few moments later. As Secretary of the Sacred College of Cardinals it would have been his duty to act as secretary of the coming conclave. It was imperative that someone be named to take his place. Cardinal Oreglia de Santo Stefano,

The Spiritual Life of Cardinal Merry del Val

Dean of the Sacred College, thought immediately of the young President of the Accademia dei Nobili Ecclesiastici and proposed his name to his fellow Cardinals. There was immediate and unanimous approval, and at the first plenary assembly they elected Archbishop Merry del Val secretary of the coming conclave. The Cardinals were all aware of his outstanding ability, but even more, as several illustrious members of the Sacred College put it, of his exceptional holiness and virtue.

The election came as a great surprise to the young Archbishop of Nicaea but he accepted it in the true spirit of obedience to the voice of God. It was the end of the scholastic year and time to leave for the summer villa with his students of the Accademia. The Archbishop was looking. forward to a few weeks of relaxation but he forgot all about that now and immediately put all his efforts into the gigantic and complex arrangements for the conclave. Although he had spent eight years in the Vatican as Papal Chamberlain on active duty with His Holiness and was well acquainted with the physical set-up of the papal buildings, preparing for a conclave still involved a tremendous amount of work.

First of all, twenty-five years had elapsed since the last conclave, when Leo XIII was elected in 1878. Then, too, the conclave of 1878 was the first after the loss of the Papal States in 1870 and could hardly be taken as a norm to follow. The method of organizing the conclave proposed by Archbishop Merry del Val, and later approved by the Sacred College, proves once again what a clear-thinking person the young prelate was and how he was certainly equal to the task assigned him.

Just as the sun was going down in the wake of an extremely hot day, July 31, 1903, the princes of the Church

From Sunrise to Noon

convened in the Sistine Chapel to begin the conclave. During those days the sole preoccupation of the Cardinal Patriarch of Venice, Giuseppe Sarto, was to vote for a worthy successor to occupy the Chair of Peter. Farthest from his mind was any notion that he himself, the humble son of lowly parents from a little town in the province of Treviso, would be the next one chosen by the Lord to bear the heavy cross of the keys of the kingdom. Then, when his name began to be mentioned he felt completely crushed. With tears in his eyes he protested his unworthiness of being Sovereign Pontiff. Openly and vehemently he declared that he could never be persuaded to accept. His tears and protestations of unworthiness merely served to convince the Sacred College more and more that he was the one to elect.

All that now remained was to persuade him to make this supreme sacrifice. On the morning of August 3rd, some of the more prominent members of the Sacred College engaged him in a lengthy conversation, trying to persuade him to accept what was the express will of the Cardinals and therefore of God. At noon that same day, by order of the Cardinal Dean, Archbishop Merry del Val paid a visit to Cardinal Sarto to beg him in the name of all the Cardinals to accept the cross the Lord was offering him.

The young prelate found the Patriarch of Venice kneeling on the marble floor of the Pauline Chapel, his head bowed in prayer. He quietly knelt down beside him and in a whisper reminded him of the consensus of the Cardinals.

"No, no," said Cardinal Sarto. "Tell the Cardinal Dean, I beg of you, that they must not consider me; ask them to do me this kindness."

Then the Cardinal buried his face in his hands and continued to pray in anguish, for he sensed that his hour of sacrifice was approaching.

The younger man arose and looked down at the bent

The Spiritual Life of Cardinal Merry del Val

head. "Courage, Your Eminence," he whispered.

That was the first time Archbishop Merry del Val had ever met the Cardinal Patriarch of Venice, who was to be elected Pope the following day. Who could possibly foresee that the future Pope and this aristocratic Anglo-Spanish prelate, at opposite poles by reason of birth and upbringing, but one in their love for the supernatural, would be brought together in mind and heart through the inscrutable designs of divine Providence?

On August 4, 1903, the humble Patriarch of Venice, with tears in his eyes and prayers on his lips, bowed his head under the weight of the papal tiara and exclaimed: "I accept the papacy as I would a cross! I am ready to do the will of God." No longer merely the lowly child of a poor working man of Riese, the obscure chaplain of Tombolo, or the poor parish priest of Salzano, he was now the Vicar of Christ. He took the name Pius X—a name full of gentleness and mildness.

The evening of that same day which saw the Cardinal of Venice invested with the supreme power, Archbishop Merry del Val made his appearance before the new Pope. He had taken care of whatever work remained to be done, and now with his characteristic refinement and respect he said to the Holy Father: "Your Holiness, tired as you are, I am afraid I must ask you to sign these letters notifying the various sovereigns and heads of states of your election."

"And you, Monsignor, are not you also tired?" replied the Pontiff with sympathy and kindness.

Then, after the papers were signed and other matters taken care of, the young secretary put all the papers on the desk in front of the Pope and said: "Now, Holy Father, my office as secretary of the conclave is over. I thank you for your kindness to me, I ask you to forgive my inefficiency and the mistakes I may have made in my official capacity,

From Sunrise to Noon

and I beg your fatherly blessing.

The Holy Father looked at him with those wonderful eyes of his and said: "What, Monsignor, do you wish to leave me? No, no! Stay with me. Please, I beg you, do this for me."

The young secretary was deeply moved and hastened to reply: "No, I have no wish to leave Your Holiness, but my office is at an end. The Secretary of State whom you will nominate will take my place and continue to direct affairs."

"Take back your papers, Monsignor," was the answer. "I beg you to continue in your office as Pro-Secretary of State until I am ready to make a decision. Out of charity do this much for me."

How could anyone help but go along with the wish of the Vicar of Christ requesting something "out of charity"? The Holy Father did not want to be left without the assistance of a prelate already experienced in the handling of affairs which were at that time entirely new to him.

The young Archbishop of Nicaea readily acquiesced and, humbly bowing his head at this latest expression of God's will, stayed on beside the Pope.

Shortly thereafter the Archbishop wrote a letter to a very dear friend and former classmate at Ushaw College, Monsignor Joseph Broadhead, in which he stated: "We have a saintly Pope. He seems very prudent and alert; he is very mild and has a charming personality." Archbishop Merry del Val had complete and perfect understanding of the soul of St. Pius X.

A few days later Pope St. Pius X sent Archbishop Merry del Val a large photograph of himself—his first as Pope—with an affectionate dedication in which he called him "Our Pro-Secretary of State," and thanking him for his valuable assistance bestowed upon him a special Apostolic Blessing.

The Secretary of State

"*It is a glorious task to work with God for the salvation of souls.*"
CARDINAL MERRY DEL VAL

II

The Secretary of State

St. Pius X was a Pope with a discerning and practical eye, and in his more than forty years in the priesthood had seen many men and many things. It did not take him long to discover in Archbishop Merry del Val the man perfectly suited for the high diplomacy of the Church; one who was at the same time a "man of God"; one whose love for justice and truth would enable him to stand beside him in the face of any problem however difficult, to win out in any encounter, and to be equal to any test put to him. On October 18, 1903, in a very ordinary and matter-of-fact way the Pope appointed him his Secretary of State and a Cardinal of the Holy Roman Church with the following letter:

MOST REVEREND AND DEAR MONSIGNOR:

> The opinion of the eminent Cardinals who chose you as secretary of the conclave, the kindness wherewith you consented to undertake during this time the duties of the Secretariate of State, and the devoted care wherewith you filled this most delicate office, oblige me to ask you to assume permanently the post of my Secretary of State. For this reason, and also to satisfy a heartfelt need of my own, and to give you a little token of my warm gratitude, in the forthcoming consistory of November 9, I shall give myself the pleasure of creating you a Cardinal of the Holy Roman Church.
>
> Moreover, I can assure you, for your own personal satisfaction, that by so doing I shall perform an act most

The Spiritual Life of Cardinal Merry del Val

pleasing and acceptable to all the members of the Sacred College. Along with me they all admire the outstandingly fine qualities the Lord has bestowed upon you, qualities which you will certainly put to the best possible use and service of the Church.

To this end, with particular affection, I impart my Apostolic benediction.

PIUS PP. X

FROM THE VATICAN
October 18, 1903

Within twenty-two days Archbishop Merry del Val was created a Cardinal and given the Titular Church of St. Praxedes. St. Pius X thus put his own stamp of approval upon the high regard and unlimited confidence which his illustrious predecessor Leo XIII had always had for Archbishop Merry del Val.

The appointment as Secretary of State of a prelate only thirty-eight years of age—a very rare occurrence in the annals of the Church—and moreover a non-Italian, surprised not a few high-ranking prelates. Their consternation disappeared, however, that same evening the appointment was made when it became known that the new Pope had told a Vatican prelate: "I appointed Monsignor Merry del Val Secretary of State because I wanted to choose someone who would be a worthy successor of Cardinal Rampolla by reason of his piety and priestly spirit."

All remaining doubt completely evaporated a few days later when it was voiced about that St. Pius X had answered the comments of a prominent Cardinal with this pointed observation: "I have chosen him because he is an expert linguist. He was born in England and educated in Belgium; he is Spanish by nationality but he has lived in Italy. He is

Secretary of State

the son of a diplomat and is a diplomat himself; he is acquainted with the problems of every country. He is very modest; he is a very holy man. He comes here every morning and informs me about all the problems of the world. I never have to make a single observation. Moreover, he does not know the meaning of the word compromise."

We think it fitting to relate here what Bishop Gallagher of Detroit, Michigan, said about the nomination of Archbishop Merry del Val as Secretary of State. Writing for his fellow countrymen and in behalf of all English-speaking countries, the Bishop wrote that Cardinal Merry del Val has shown the English-speaking world that high papal offices are filled by men well versed in diplomacy, to be sure, but first and foremost by those motivated by an intense love for Christ and the Church.

He continued to say that non-Catholics probably thought that Cardinal Merry del Val's noble birth, his associations with England and Spain, his perfect knowledge of so many European languages and of diplomacy, not to mention his superior intelligence, were the chief reasons why St. Pius X decided to make him his Secretary of State. But St. Pius X, being holy himself, appointed him Secretary of State because he recognized the fact that he was a man of God, completely dedicated to the service of the divinely instituted Church, and because his spiritual life was in perfect harmony with that of the Pope himself.

The words of the Bishop of Detroit show what great esteem the new Cardinal enjoyed everywhere, but at the same time they serve as an acknowledgment of St. Pius X's great intuition and sanctity.

That Cardinal Merry del Val did not know the meaning of the word compromise"—high praise indeed—was brought out quite clearly in the conclave when his attention was drawn to the fact that Cardinal Puzyna, Bishop of Krakow,

The Spiritual Life of Cardinal Merry del Val

intended to invoke Austria's "veto" against Cardinal Rampolla. Respectfully, but none the less firmly, the young secretary pointed out several reasons why it should not be done and succeeded in getting him to drop the matter.

The Holy Father's words summed up the matter quite clearly. No one could or would now dare to question the appointment of the new Secretary of State. Actually the young Cardinal had tried to refuse the high honor and arduous assignment just a few days before it was made public. He accepted, however, when he heard the Holy Father make the almost prophetic pronouncement: "Accept. It is the will of God. We will work and suffer together out of love for the Church."

To work and suffer for the Church! What a program, replete with challenges and heartache! It is, of course, none other than that which Our Blessed Lord Himself mapped out for His Apostles when He sent them out in search for souls.

This was the new Pope's way of saying "Thanks" for the bit of encouragement whispered so sympathetically into his ear by the young secretary of the conclave.

Cardinal Merry del Val now knew what God wanted of him. The last bit of doubt had been dispelled by the direct and beautiful words of the Sovereign Pontiff. With eyes fixed on the suffering and sorrow promised him by the new Vicar of Christ, he undertook the difficult task. It was one that could have discouraged even a man of more mature age and far greater experience if suddenly called upon to fill such a high office.

From that day and that hour on, he worked side by side with a Pope who had come up from an environment totally different from his own. He belonged no longer to himself but to the Church, and for eleven uninterrupted years, with no vacillation of any sort, he suffered, prayed, and fought. His name and work were synonymous with the name and work

Secretary of State

of St. Pius X. They felt and thought along identical lines; they had but one goal, one faith, and one spirit animating all their actions. In large measure Cardinal Merry del Val bore the weight of the formidable task of "restoring all things in Christ," which the Holy Father, with absolute confidence in assistance from above, had taken upon himself as the supernatural program of his pontificate.

On February 27, 1930, one of the better-known newspapers of Germany, the *Freiburger Tagespost* wrote as follows:

"It is hard to determine up to what point the unusually fruitful reign of Pius X was the work of that Pontiff and how much his Secretary of State had to do with it. This much is certain: if the reign of Pius X is called the pontificate of important and decisive religious reforms, then Cardinal Merry del Val had a lot to do with bringing it about through the generous and effective contribution he made in his never-ending work."

Let us merely say that Cardinal Merry del Val was not only an intelligent and capable minister carrying out the thoughts and wishes of St. Pius X, but also a faithful collaborator harmonizing perfectly with the mind and will of the Pope.

This fact can be proved conclusively from testimony furnished by the Holy Father himself. After the customary audience granted the Secretary of State every morning, whenever St. Pius X had to consult him on urgent matters, so as not to take him away from his work he used to send him written messages and would ask for an opinion or advice. In many of these notes can be found phrases or expressions that clearly show how loyally and devotedly the Cardinal worked day after day in perfect harmony with his

The Spiritual Life of Cardinal Merry del Val

sovereign. They furnish us with proof of the Cardinal's complete devotion to duty, his utter disdain for popular opinion or praise, his absolute lack of any servile fear which so often characterizes, as St. Catherine of Siena once remarked, the actions of those in high positions of honor and responsibility.

Just a few excerpts from these messages of Pope St. Pius X will be enough to prove our point:

"Your Eminence, I agree wholeheartedly with the advice you have given."

"Your Eminence, do not be unduly upset. Whatever happens, the responsibility is not only yours but mine too and we shall share it together in peace. I await the opinion of Your Eminence: an opinion you may give me at your convenience and one that will most certainly be greatly appreciated."

Further proof of the Cardinal's faithful collaboration with St. Pius X can be found in the delicate sentiments of gratitude and affection which the Pope manifested from time to time in his correspondence with the Secretary of State.

On August 11, 1904, the Pope wrote: "I find it difficult to express my gratitude for your generous manifestations of affection carried to the point of sacrifice that you constantly shower upon me. As long as the Lord sees fit to leave me here below, I pray that He may grant me the grace of having you always close

On August 20, 1905: "I thank you for the way you never fail to think of me and the Vatican, but be assured, none the less, that there is nothing I wish for more than your good health. The well-being of Your Eminence has a wonderful influence on my morale and my own physical condition."

On January 1, 1913, he sent the Cardinal a little gift and

Secretary of State

with it the following message of esteem and affection: "I hope you will accept this little token of my gratitude for the wise and disinterested help you offer me; for the many sacrifices you make for me in the government of the Church."

St. Pius X's high regard for the work done by his Secretary of State is also brought out in a letter he wrote on September 7, 1904, to the President of the Economic Union of Catholics in Italy. He wrote as follows: "Because of my high regard for His Eminence the Cardinal Secretary of State, who is not in Rome at the moment, I would not like to make any decision without first consulting him."

Another indication of how much help Cardinal Merry del Val gave through perfect collaboration with the Pope is furnished by the personal letters in which St. Pius X would send him greetings and best wishes every year on his feast day. It would be hard to find a more sincere and outspoken acknowledgment of the perfect cooperation given the Pope by "his own" Cardinal, as he liked to call him.

Actually, whenever the Holy Father talked about him he found it hard to conceal his satisfaction at having him by his side, saying time and again that "he could not thank the Lord enough for having given him such a valuable assistant and co-worker."

Camillus Bellaigue, well-known author and Private Chamberlain of His Holiness, made the following pertinent observation:

"All during the reign of the saintly Pope Pius X, I was thrown into contact with Cardinal Merry del Val. His intelligence was on a par with the nobility of his soul. To the best of my ability I tried to be of service to this outstanding servant of a truly great master. And just like his master, I too loved him. I can still hear Pius X saying: 'Be separated

The Spiritual Life of Cardinal Merry del Val

from Cardinal Merry del Val? Why, it would be easier to cut off Our head. How could We possibly get along without him?'"

On March 20, 1916, almost two years after the death of the saintly Pope, the French author Charles Belin wrote the following: "'My own Merry,' Pius X used to say, when speaking of His Secretary of State, thus emphasizing the great bond of intimacy which the heart had forged between sovereign and devoted minister, between father and loving son, who now in turn, speaking of the Pope whom he mourns, says: 'My own Pius X.'"

The eleven years which the Cardinal spent side by side with St. Pius X were filled to the brim with sharp encounters and bitter conflicts, for it was at a time when Christianity was the target of all sorts of secular laws and scheming, of bitter anticlerical prohibitions, of upheavals among the intelligentsia, and of outright rejection of the supernatural element in our daily life. This all meant hard work and no end of responsibility, but the Cardinal applied himself with courage and fortitude, fully aware that he was paving the way for future conquests and ultimate victory on the part of Holy Mother Church.

Before the close of his life, St. Pius X enjoyed the great satisfaction of being able to see how much his vigorous work of reform had actually accomplished. The hierarchy was once more solidly united with the Chair of Peter and the clergy had been made fully aware of the responsibility of its divine mission. Where before the Catholic laity had been torn by discord and rebellion, it was now obedient to the commands of the Vicar of Christ. The primacy of the supernatural was reaffirmed and put into practice in the face of vicious theories and cleverly disguised heretical ideas. These latter errors had distorted the Christian way of living, but St. Pius X pursued them relentlessly, brought them out

Secretary of State

into the open, and then condemned them.

Now this much we can safely say: all these glorious achievements on the part of one of the most illustrious and forceful Pontiffs the Church has ever had are intimately connected with the name and collaboration of Cardinal Merry del Val. With love and loyalty beyond measure he knew how to interpret the mind and will, the thoughts and directives of his sovereign.

The Cardinal's aim was "certainly not that of adding any luster to his own accomplishments," as the future Pius XII pointed out, "but merely of letting the world know about and admire the vital and forceful action of the Vicar of Christ."

For eleven years the Cardinal was "one heart and one mind" with his Pope, in everything that happened and under all kinds of circumstances, in joy and in sorrow. Working and living with the Pope on the same high supernatural level, the Cardinal had the consolation of being right beside him when he closed his eyes in death.

The evening of August 14, 1914, was a sad one indeed for Rome and the whole Catholic world. The big bell of St. Peter's tolled mournfully letting the people of Rome know that the saintly Pope was in his death agony. All the bells of Rome took up the sad call and soon the churches were full of people. It was an hour of heartbreak and sadness for the world, torn asunder as it was by the ravages of the First World War, but for the dying Pope it was an hour of heavenly beauty and splendor as he murmured words of supplication, self-immolation, and of peace.

Completely broken up with grief, Cardinal Merry del Val had hurried immediately to the bedside of the dying Pontiff. The saintly old man had lost the power of speech but his mind was still calm and clear. He fixed his penetrating gaze

The Spiritual Life of Cardinal Merry del Val

on the eyes of his Cardinal Secretary of State; then he stretched out his pale hands in a silent and touching farewell. He took hold of the Cardinal's hands, squeezed them tightly and held on to them for a long while, almost as if he wanted to tell him how tenderly he loved him. It was his way of expressing the depth of his gratitude, his final stamp of approval, his "Consummatum est" placed upon their work and sacrifice.

Even before the first light of dawn broke over the city of Rome, the saintly Pope lay resting in the peace of death.

Great beyond measure was the grief of Cardinal Merry del Val. On September 9, less than a month after the Pope's death, the Cardinal wrote to a parish priest in Umbria: "I am completely broken up with grief over the death of my angelic Pontiff and father, Pius X. I have suffered and continue to suffer so very, very much." He also wrote to an old and dear friend in England, Monsignor Broadhead: "The blow has been a terrible one for me, and my heart is fairly broken. You see, I loved him with every fiber of my soul; and I feel as if I could not live without him."

That same day he answered a letter of the future Cardinal Masella: "You undoubtedly can appreciate how much I have been broken up with grief over the death of my holy Pontiff and father, Pius X. It seems impossible for me to go on living without him and I shall mourn his death all the rest of my life."

These sentiments of undying love and loyalty to "his" Pope kept recurring in his mind and heart and came to the surface again on the second anniversary of the death of St. Pius X.

On August 19, 1916, he wrote a letter to Ermenegilda Parolin, a niece who had been greatly attached to her uncle, St. Pius X, that shows he felt his grief as keenly then as ever: "My thoughts these days turn more than ever to the memory

Secretary of State

of our dearly beloved and esteemed Holy Father Pius X. The months and years go by but my grief over having lost him is just as great and as much alive today as ever."

This "intense grief that knew no end" was robbed of some of its bitterness by the consolation he found in his pious pilgrimages to the native countryside of the saintly Pontiff.

A stone in the façade of the home of the niece and nephew of St. Pius X, solemnly dedicated on September 21, 1933, commemorates the Cardinal's four visits to Riese. On the occasion of his last visit to the little house where St. Pius X was born, next to his name in the register of visitors he wrote the words: "Always in my thoughts, forever in my heart."

He derived a measure of comfort also from the affection he always felt for the humble parents of St. Pius X. It served to make him a part of their little pleasures and joys as well as their domestic troubles and sorrow.

Immediately after St. Pius X had given his last testament of love and gratitude, Cardinal Merry del Val left the Vatican, as serene and unperturbed as ever. He silently crossed the threshold of the quiet and unpretentious Palazzo Santa Marta. This modest little house was the traditional home of the Cardinal Archpriest of St. Peter's Basilica and was located in the Piazza della Sacrestia, just a stone's throw from St. Peter's. This house formerly stood directly in front of the Roman Minor Seminary, which was later converted into the Palace of Justice of Vatican City, at which time Santa Marta's was torn down.

Cardinal Merry del Val spent many years there all alone with his wonderful and unforgettable memories of the saintly Pontiff, always in the hope that he might live to see them enshrined in the grateful hearts of mankind. He left

The Spiritual Life of Cardinal Merry del Val

the limelight to lead a life of obscurity for the sole purpose of drawing closer to God. He had retired from the world of the mighty and influential, but certainly not from the vast multitude of the humble and lowly whom he loved dearly and by whom he was loved just as much in return.

The Cardinal returned to the greatest temple of Christianity as its Archpriest and nothing more. Actually, St. Pius X, a few months before his death, had wanted to make him Archpriest because he felt sure by so doing that he would be giving St. Peter's Basilica one who through his piety could edify both clergy and faithful. Moreover, he knew that the Cardinal with his exquisite artistic taste would be able to add new luster to the tomb of the First Vicar of Christ.

The former Secretary of State continued his work on the seventeen Sacred Congregations and Pontifical Commissions to which he belonged. Everyone there had such high regard for his opinions and sage advice, not to mention his vast experience, that a well-known churchman once described him as a "born teacher."

He continued to function as an eminent orator with world-wide appeal. His thoughts were always so deep and clear and delivered with such masterful eloquence that he never failed to stir up profound admiration in his listeners. As bishop and prince of the Church, his deep faith and piety, supplemented by his virile and noble priestly carriage, served to add a more solemn tone to the splendor of the sacred rites and solemn functions.

As a spiritual director he was in a class by himself. Above all else he remained a humble priest of God with his eyes fixed upon eternity. In complete possession of an untroubled conscience, he lived day by day an intense supernatural life. Written in the little notebook that served as a diary for the innermost secrets and aspirations of his

Secretary of State

soul were the words he kept constantly before his mind: "Find God in the sanctifying prose of daily duty—silence and recollection—prayer and activity—sacrifice and love."

Many memorable events took place during this last period of the life of Cardinal Merry del Val. June 28, 1923, was certainly a day never to be forgotten when beneath the vast dome of St. Peter's Basilica he witnessed the erection of a monument to Pius X, made possible by contributions from Catholics all over the world. His saintly Pontiff came alive again before his eyes in that carved marble with all the majestic solemnity of his papal robes and the tiara resting on his head.

On June 25, 1925, the Cardinal celebrated his silver jubilee as a bishop. He was still enjoying perfect health but, after all, he was very young to be commemorating twenty-five years in the episcopacy. Actually, his jubilee fell on May 6, 1925, but since his mother had died just five days before that date he postponed his celebration until the following June.

On that day all vied with one another in manifesting their admiration and respect for the Cardinal, beginning with the reigning Pope Pius XI. "We well know," wrote the Holy Father, "with what fidelity you served our predecessor of immortal memory, Leo XIII, working at his side as Private Chamberlain, or exercising in his name and with his authority more than an ordinary legation, or directing the education of the students of the Noble Ecclesiastical Academy. In discharging these affairs you gave such proof of care, diligence, and prudence as to induce Pius X, when he had scarcely ascended the Chair of St. Peter, to elevate you to the Cardinalate, and to entrust you with the negotiations of the public interests of the Church."

The Holy Father wanted this letter delivered personally to Cardinal Merry del Val by his own Secretary of State,

The Spiritual Life of Cardinal Merry del Val

Cardinal Gasparri, to make it quite clear to all that he had only the highest regard and esteem for the Secretary of State of St. Pius X.

Cardinals, governors, heads of states, bishops, prelates, and eminent personages all followed suit in their expression of esteem. Personal friends and admirers and, of course, just ordinary, every-day people in large numbers were on hand to congratulate him. His celebration certainly reflected the prestige and universal respect which were attached to his name.

Twice he served as representative of the Vicar of Christ at the tomb of St. Francis of Assisi. The first time was on October 1, 1920, for the centenary of the discovery of the body of St. Francis.

Much greater solemnity, in keeping with the change in times and circumstances, marked his second visit in 1926 for the seventh centenary of the death of the Poverello. It was this second visit as Papal Legate to the land "completely seraphic in fervor" which resulted in a truly wonderful happening in the contemporary history of the Church and Italy. On the memorable morning of October 4, 1926, with the beautiful frescos of Giotto serving as a background for the magnificence of the sacred ceremonies, Cardinal Merry del Val sat majestically on the papal throne looking out on a vast multitude of people. In the presence of the Prime Minister of Italy, with a voice vibrating with deep feeling and emotion, he called down upon Italy the self-same blessing St. Francis had invoked on his beloved city under similar circumstances back in 1226.

That historic blessing, as it fell from the lips of the Papal Legate, seemed to stand out as a sign and token of better and more peaceful things to come and was well received on all sides. It marked the climax of those efforts toward peace and harmony which he himself during the reign of St. Pius X had

Secretary of State

gotten under way with his "Instructions to the Bishops of Italy." In them he made unmistakably clear the thought of the Apostolic See and settled once and for all the position of Italian Catholics as citizens. Thus would be eventually born the union between the Rome of the Caesars and the Rome of Peter.

Another memorable date in the life of the Cardinal was November 9, 1928, when he celebrated his silver jubilee as a Cardinal. This event attracted much attention at Rome and throughout the entire Catholic world. For little by little, as his personality and accomplishments began to emerge from the shadow of strictly contemporary events, they assumed greater magnitude and were now being viewed in the proper light of Church history.

It would be an impossible task to mention the many letters and telegrams Cardinal Merry del Val received on that occasion, expressing regard and wishing him well. We can, however, quote from a letter of Cardinal Salotti, which sums up the sentiments generally expressed:

YOUR EMINENCE:

Your jubilee as a Cardinal assumes particular significance because it serves to remind us of the great trust placed in you by a saintly Pontiff, and at the same time of your many merits acquired over a span of twenty-five years spent working zealously as a prince of the Church within the very shadow of the Vatican.

Now just twenty-five years from the day when Pius X made Your Eminence a member of the illustrious senate of the Church, we are in a better position to appreciate the action taken by that Pope in selecting you as the perfect collaborator for his vast work of reform, reform which has since produced so much good fruit for religion as well as for society. By celebrating, therefore, the date of your jubilee as a Cardinal, we honor history

The Spiritual Life of Cardinal Merry del Val

and pay due homage to the truth. This is what I have in mind as I extend to you my best wishes and congratulations, making them one with all those you have already received from Catholics all over the world.

At sixty-four years of age Cardinal Merry del Val was still apparently in good health and vigorously active. Watching him take his walks through the streets of Rome, or seeing him preside at the solemn functions in St. Peter's, always so erect and attentive, or even to hear him carry on a conversation with all the vigor of a young man, one would have said that this man would surely live to a ripe old age. Instead, his life was almost over. As a matter of fact, the Cardinal seemed to have some sort of premonition that death was near.

In the Vatican City at that time they were busy working on a new residence for the Cardinal Archpriest of St. Peter's. In giving the news to a friend of his in England, he wrote: "My new home as Archpriest will be bigger and more comfortable but I don't know whether I'll ever live there."

He sent his brother in Spain a photograph of the new building, still under construction, and said: "This will be my home if I live long enough to make use of it."

Another day as he stood at his window in the old building of Santa Marta a distinguished visitor from England was there with him. Pointing to the new construction the Cardinal remarked: "Maybe I'll die before seeing it completed!"

Every time he talked about his new home, he would add: "Who knows what might happen; I doubt if I'll be here to see it finished." He used to keep telling those with whom he was in daily contact: "The only thing left for me now is the

Secretary of State

tomb." Was it premonition or merely a longing on his part for a better and more glorious life?

He was stricken with sudden illness; it came upon him unexpectedly. The same could certainly not be said, however, of death which followed in its wake.

On the morning of February 20, 1930, he had celebrated Mass at the tomb of St. Pius X in the Vatican crypt, as was his custom on the twentieth day of every month, the day when the Pontiff had gone to his eternal reward. On the twenty-third, a Sunday, he went over to St. Peter's twice in the discharge of his ministry; he conferred the diaconate on a member of the clergy attached to the basilica and then administered Confirmation and First Holy Communion to a captain in the army. Later on in the day, at the express wish of His Holiness, he baptized the little daughter of Marquis Edward Persichetti-Ugolini and Mary Louise Ratti, a niece of the Holy Father.

The afternoon of the twenty-fourth, together with his ever-faithful Monsignor Canali, he took a brisk walk through Trastevere to his beloved Association of the Sacred Heart of Jesus. He seemed very well then, but when he got home he complained about feeling a bit upset. About ten o'clock that night he went into his private chapel and prayed for a long while with head bowed down between his hands like one completely absorbed in the things of eternity.

The next day there was some uncertainty about the ailment that was destined to take his life. Then a sudden attack of appendicitis called for an immediate operation. With his customary serenity and self-composure the Cardinal murmured: "I am in the hands of God." Then he remained silent as though absorbed in profound and sublime meditation.

It was natural enough for him not to be upset about death or its imminence. His little diary contained many

The Spiritual Life of Cardinal Merry del Val

comforting reflections about death; for example: "To die means closing your eyes and falling asleep; then waking up in heaven." "Tranquillity is the all-important thing at the moment of death, keeping in mind that you are going from this life to the other as you would through a door opening up to lead you to God."

He was calm and sure of himself, just as he had been when he wrote in his last will and testament: "I lovingly accept death when and how God shall will, in expiation for my sins and adoring His divine decree."

How could he help being serene considering that just a month or so before his death, he made the following observation in a letter: "My life is practically over and I have to be ready for God's call. If there could be any sadness in heaven, it would be because there is nothing more up there to be done for Jesus."

He was calm because his hands were full of goodness and virtue, because with the Apostle of the Gentiles, he too could say: "I have fought the good fight" (2 Tim. 4,7). Like Simeon he could humbly beg the Lord to let him sing: "Now Thou dost dismiss Thy servant," and be ushered into a glory that knows no shadow, into a light of day without sunset, and the blinding vision of Almighty God. When his hour came, it was a pious and holy death. He passed away silently and without any agony in the afternoon of February 26, 1930. His farewell message had already been written; he had prepared it a few months before, on July 19, 1929. It stands out like a beautiful sunset at the end of his hard working-day.

"On my tomb let there be written only my name and these words: 'Give me souls; take away all else,' the aspiration of my whole life.

"I ask pardon of all those whom I may have offended, and I implore the mercy of God, grieving that I have not

Secretary of State

served Him better.

"I bless my dear sons of Trastevere, and the Communities whose Protector I am, and I recommend myself to their prayers."

He left his episcopal cross to the Holy Father as a final token of his loyalty to the Vicar of Christ and of his absolute devotion to the See of Peter.

He bequeathed all he possessed to the Sacred Congregation of the Propagation of the Faith on behalf of poor missions in pagan lands. Not a single earthly thought entered the picture: no preoccupation for his relatives; no concern about his nephews. His only thought and sole concern was the salvation of souls. From the beginning to the end of his life it was: "Give me souls; take away all else."

As soon as the sad news of Cardinal Merry del Val's death became known in the gathering dusk, a large number of people of all ages and from every walk of life made their way to the Palazzo Santa Marta to give vent to their deep sorrow and grief. Cardinals, prelates of the Vatican, bishops and priests, diplomats and students, soldiers, and ordinary day-laborers still in their working clothes, knelt down with reverence before his body while his dear sons of Trastevere kept watch beside it. As Cardinal Canali stated: "The people who came to say a prayer before the mortal remains of the Cardinal were certainly not less than twelve thousand and they presented a touching picture of piety, admiration, and gratitude."

Big and little alike paid homage to the deceased Cardinal: the former, to a man who knew how to be big among the big, a true nobleman by birth and training, a nobleman in the highest sense of the word by reason of his uncommon virtue and holiness; the latter in like manner paid their respects to a prelate who, for thirty years, through

The Spiritual Life of Cardinal Merry del Val

his charity had been within the reach of the poor and lowly, comforting and helping them in their needs, consoling them in their troubles, and guiding them constantly in the practice of virtue.

The Cardinal who had lived side by side with a saintly Pontiff had expressed a wish that he be put to rest near the tomb of "his" Pope in the Vatican crypt. Before God and man it would thus be an unspoken tribute to the faith and love with which he had served his master from that bright August 4, 1903, to August 20, 1914, which marked the sunset of "his" Pope's mortal life.

The pious Cardinal whom God had raised to the very peak of power and glory had this final wish granted him. On the morning of March 3rd, his sons from Trastevere lifted up his body and carried it in silence from the Palazzo Santa Marta to the Vatican crypt. On hand were members of the Sacred College and the papal court, of the diplomatic corps and the Roman aristocracy, followed by an immense multitude of people. In the darkness of the Vatican crypt they saw his body laid to rest at the feet of his beloved sovereign, his final act of love, loyalty, and devotion.

His own tomb already had become the object of devout prayers and heartfelt piety. At that moment he ceased to be a prominent figure in contemporary history and started to assume even greater proportions for countless souls who had felt and understood the holiness of his life.

Not only Rome, accustomed as it is to great events and outstanding prelates, but practically the whole world was deeply affected by the death of St. Pius X's Secretary of State. All felt that with his passing away the Sacred College had lost one of its most illustrious members, a man who, by the sanctity of his active life, had shed great luster on the Cardinalate, the Church and the Catholic world.

Secretary of State

Rome went into deep mourning and paid homage to the memory of the priest and Cardinal who for forty uninterrupted years had gone down among the poor people of the City and tried to assist them.

The international press, regardless of creed or political affiliation, hastened to add its spontaneous tribute of admiration for the deceased Cardinal. It singled out the spotlessness of his character and his great loyalty to Pius X; his outstanding accomplishments as well as his unblemished personal life. He was eulogized and mourned everywhere: in Italy and England; in France, Switzerland, and Luxemburg; in Spain, Austria, and Germany; in Canada and the United States; in Latin America and far-off China.

Such an impressive demonstration of grief and universal mourning took place only because, as one newspaper put it: "A great man had disappeared and together with him the memory of an unforgettable era in the history of the Church and the world."

St. Pius X's loyal Secretary of State had written in his will: "I desire to be buried with the utmost simplicity." But Spain, the land of his ancestors, expressed the desire to make his last resting place a tomb of onyx from the Balearic Islands. So, on the morning of July 11, 1931, this tomb was dedicated with a beautiful discourse by His Eminence, Cardinal Eugenio Pacelli, Secretary of State to His Holiness and Archpriest of the Vatican Basilica. Before a large gathering the future Pius XII spoke as follows:

> This tomb is a glorious monument that does honor to Catholic Spain which has so generously desired to enclose the revered mortal remains of its illustrious son, Cardinal Merry del Val, in this magnificent yet strikingly plain sarcophagus of precious onyx from its famous mines of Majorca. It serves to remind us that the only

The Spiritual Life of Cardinal Merry del Val

true greatness here below is to be found in holy simplicity of the soul and in the brightness of virtue that covers it with merit in the eyes of God. At the same time, however, this tomb reminds Spain that the heroes honoring her most and adding to her glory are those, her children, who boasted and were proud of the way they defended the Catholic faith. This is what constitutes Spain's true greatness, and among the many such stars of first magnitude there shines the figure of Cardinal Merry del Val. His whole life was a brilliant reflection of those virtues which have always been the outstanding characteristic of the Spanish people—courage, faith, fortitude under fire, serenity in times of trouble, and unsurpassable loyalty.

This tomb, he went on to say, is entrusted to the care of the Vatican Chapter. But there is a much more powerful Hand that keeps watch over it down here, sheltered as it is in the shadow of this venerable and ancient crypt, the cradle of resurrection for so many Pontiffs, Cardinals, and princes over whose mortal remains gently stirs that same breath of hope which caresses the sacred remains of the First Vicar of Christ, the rock and foundation of the Catholic Church. And in the circle of these many tombs, that of Cardinal Merry del Val carries an inspiration all its own by reason of his association with the Pontiff Pius X of holy memory, by whose side he suffered, fought, and prayed so much that it was said of the Cardinal that, rather than an executive minister, he seemed to be a trusted and intimate collaborator in the government of the Church.

These two great souls have certainly met again in the sight of God and have been reunited to enjoy the reward of their work. Their names will be forever a part of history and linked together in the splendor of the light of truth and peace which the Roman papacy shed

Secretary of State

upon the world during the first decades of this century. Moreover, it is so beautiful and inspiring to *see* their tombs here side by side as they take their eternal rest, the two of them who lived and worked together for such a long period of time.

Nevertheless in this tomb [concluded His Eminence], like one tired of sleeping the lips of Cardinal Merry del Val continue to move; they conquer death through the words written on the sarcophagus, crying out incessantly to God: "Give me souls; take away all else." It is the cry of his faith and his zeal and by it "though he is dead, he yet speaks" (Hebr. 11, 4). It was his thirst for souls that set his heart afire and broadened it so as to embrace all, those near to as well as far from truth and virtue. It was his thirst for souls that took him down among the poor people of Rome even when he was an eminent prince of the Church. This thirst will now be perpetuated in the aforementioned words, and let all know who kneel before the cold stone now shrouding his priestly, worn-out heart just how much it was on fire with the Spirit of Christ who, through His Passion and Precious Blood, had taught him the inestimable value of souls. In these words we find the summation of his mortal career as well as the pledge of his immortal glory.

Spain had given a tomb to the illustrious Cardinal of Spanish descent. The Catholics of England, land of his birth, erected at the entrance to the sacristy in St. Peter's a carved marble portrait of the Cardinal.

His Eminence Cardinal Pacelli, accompanied by all those who had assisted at the dedication of the tomb, left the Vatican crypt and proceeded to the ambulatory leading from the basilica into the sacristy. The procession stopped in front of the marble memorial and there Monsignor Theodore Heard, an Auditor of the Holy Roman Rota, delivered the

The Spiritual Life of Cardinal Merry del Val

following address in the name of his fellow English Catholics:

> It is indeed a great distinction for me to present this marble memorial in honor of the esteemed Cardinal Merry del Val. The sudden and irreparable loss of such an illustrious and great prince of the Church almost immediately prompted some of his friends and admirers in England to take action toward erecting this memorial in his honor out of their own personal contributions. Other pious people then joined in the collection as did other countries too, out of friendship or admiration for the Cardinal.
>
> The medallion being unveiled today shows the Cardinal with his face turned toward the basilica, and we think a lesson can be drawn from this. It can be interpreted as a paternal invitation to all of us to follow him to church and join with him in prayer, and with the same sentiments of faith, humility, and religious fervor enter into this greatest temple of Christianity in which he shed so much luster and edified people from all over the world by his impressive dignity and composure, by his extraordinary holiness of life.

Then His Eminence Cardinal Pacelli began to speak, first pointing out how much Cardinal Merry del Val loved the country of his birth, then briefly outlining his burning apostolic zeal in leading so many souls groping in darkness to the light and the ways of truth.

> Our deceased Cardinal's thoughts were constantly directed toward his brethren who had strayed from the truth. He used to pray for them himself and would get the young men of his beloved "Association of Trastevere" to do the same. In both public and private

Secretary of State

conversation, as also with the written word, he made every effort to remove all obstacles, to pave the way for their return to the center of the unity of faith. Think of the many souls who under his paternal and wise guidance found themselves once more a part of the sheepfold of Christ! His portrait, therefore, decorating this ambulatory stands as a memorial to him and his work. It is at the same time a monument expressing the gratitude of all who admired his charity in going out to look for souls and lead them back to God, of all who were the direct object of his paternal affection and wise counsel.

Portrait of a Man

"It is for us to reflect as in a mirror the light of Him Who is the true light; but the mirror must be clean and pure."
CARDINAL MERRY DEL VAL

III

Portrait of a Man

TO UNDERSTAND fully Cardinal Merry del Val's spirituality we have to consider it against the solid background of his human personality. The supernatural in him blended perfectly with those physical and moral attributes that nature had bestowed upon him. Perfect balance and harmony resulted in much the same way that shadow in contrast with light serves to make the figures in a picture stand out.

The Cardinal's nobility of birth was matched by that of his soul; he was a prince of the Church yet a servant of God; although a diplomat he remained none the less the priest of God. From his mother he inherited Anglo-Saxon characteristics—a well-disciplined firmness, a measured appreciation of life, and extreme tenaciousness. From his father he received his noble blood, and with it the mentality, daring, and courage that are typical of Latin races.

The Cardinal was tall and erect, with noble features; he had a broad forehead and piercing eyes. There was something majestic and regal about his walk. The splendor of his Cardinal's robes lent a solemnity to his person that was almost unbelievable. More than one discerning observer remarked that "He looked like someone straight out of a picture from the Renaissance."

The description fitted him perfectly. The French writer Bertrin made the following observation: "You would have to be a Van Dyke or a Velasquez to draw a picture of Cardinal Merry del Val. He speaks several languages with amazing ability and precision. The pleasantness and refinement of his speech, the aristocratic courtesy of his manners, his whole appearance so full of dignity and decorum immediately

The Spiritual Life of Cardinal Merry del Val

make an impression upon a visitor, and he soon realizes he is in the presence of a man of great stature, one gifted with a strong and unwavering determination to further the welfare of the Church."

A Canadian, writing in the *Catholic Register* of Toronto, February 15, 1912, made this remark about the Cardinal, then Secretary of State: "He presents a beautiful picture of a man; he seems born to wear the purple. He impresses you at first sight and the impression grows every time you see him. He is the perfect model of a court prelate and, in my opinion, the most outstanding member of the Sacred College. In the Sistine Chapel I saw him bringing the Pope his ring during the ceremony of the consecration: he was the center of attraction and admiration on the part of all."

An American correspondent saw the Cardinal pontificate in the beautiful Church of St. Ignatius at Rome on May 13, 1924, at the centenary of the restoration of the Gregorian University and wrote as follows: "Seated on his throne in all the splendor of the liturgy, Cardinal Merry del Val created a wonderful impression and made you think of the majesty, grandeur, and universality of the Church."

On February 28, 1930, the *New York Herald* carried the following eulogy: "Aristocratic and cosmopolitan, Cardinal Merry del Val could well be compared with any of the great ecclesiastical figures or men of the past. He was a wonderful example of that power which the Catholic Church still possesses and has always possessed through the centuries: the power of attracting to herself the best minds both in the field of organization as well as in that of politics of any and every age."

On March 19, 1930, New York's *Commonweal* carried an article on the Cardinal written by its editor, Michael Williams:

Portrait of a Man

"In a world almost overwhelmed by mediocrities, it is high consolation to meet such men as the late Spanish-Irish Cardinal. . . Mother Church, it seems to me, had brought into complete harmony the most admirable and distinctive traits of a cultured gentleman. He was an example of that true aristocracy which has been nourished by the Catholic Church throughout the centuries: an aristocracy of talent, or of genius, or of service, which chooses its leaders from any rank or class of men or women, and gives their native gifts or acquirements the fullest possible development and opportunity to manifest themselves."

Like all truly great men, the Cardinal's dignity was one of his most attractive qualities. "When he passed through the streets of Rome," wrote the French author Rene Bazin, "everyone used to admire him; they would look at him with interest and take great pleasure in greeting him."
He was a tall and majestic-looking man, and when he made an appearance at St. Peter's with all the splendor of the basilica and the magnificence of the sacred ceremonies serving as a background he almost seemed to cast a spell of enchantment around about him.

In the words of an internationally known man of letters: "Anyone who ever had the privilege of seeing the Cardinal's majestic figure at the altar raising his hand to impart a blessing or heard his high and solemn voice in the chant of the sacred liturgy, could never forget it. The man, his personality, and his voice were eminently worthy of this place, unlike any other in the world, and blended perfectly with the fascination the basilica at certain times exerts upon all, young and old, ignorant and learned, believers and unbelievers of every nation."
After seeing the Cardinal as celebrant at one of the

The Spiritual Life of Cardinal Merry del Val

sacred functions at St. Peter's, Paul Boyer, a distinguished French lawyer, summed up his impressions: "I shall never forget the majestic appearance of this strikingly handsome Cardinal presiding at solemn services in the Vatican Basilica. When talking to him in his parlor, he was exactly the same as he was on those memorable occasions in St. Peter's."

Miss Annie Beauregard-Bowe of Philadelphia got the same sort of impression. She stated: "The Vatican Basilica holds an indescribable fascination for all Catholics. But we who have seen His Eminence pontificate at the altar of the cathedral can truthfully say that he formed an integral part of the beauty of this wonderful temple."

Cardinal Merry del Val was a dynamic student and scholar. One of his professors at the Gregorian University said: "In the solitude of the Palazzo Santa Marta with its treasure of wonderful memories, where there still lingered the sweet fragrance of the virtues of his great predecessor, Cardinal Rampolla, he used to study and ponder over his more difficult problems. His opinions and decisions were perfect models of clarity and logic; there were depth and richness in his doctrine."

A learned Dominican, Father Marco Sales, Master of the Sacred Apostolic Palaces, had no hesitation about testifying: "The Cardinal was thoroughly acquainted with the most complex and important political, religious, and social problems of the international world. Theology, Sacred Scripture, philosophy, history, apologetics, sociology, and diplomacy were all in his field of activity."

This opinion was fully endorsed by many high-ranking scholars who recognized the Cardinal's extraordinary competence, particularly in the field of Biblical studies. After all, who could ever forget those memorable controversies on the authenticity, historicity, and divine inspiration of the

Portrait of a Man

Holy Books, so viciously attacked by Modernism under the guise of subjecting the Bible to a positive and objective critique?

The aforementioned editor of *Commonweal*, Michael Williams, goes on to say in his article: "He summed up the education and culture of Catholic Europe. As a journalist I have interviewed many of the great ones of this world. But Cardinal Merry del Val occupies a place apart from all others by virtue of the high degree of serene, mellow, yet ardent cosmopolitan culture which distinguished him. He was a reminder of the great standards which once ruled our western civilization."

One of the representative churchmen of France made this statement: "The Cardinal possessed a clear and positive knowledge of facts; he knew how to analyze and coordinate them. Above all, he knew how to sum them up and draw out the general ideas. He possessed this distinctive quality to a very high degree. In this respect he was, better than anyone else, familiar with the conditions and activity of the Church in every country, its needs, deficiencies, and dangers. This was frequently brought to my attention especially with regard to what concerned France."

He read a great deal, including the leading newspapers and magazines, both Italian and foreign; he followed attentively the development of modern thought, the various movements of Protestantism in all parts of the world.

Nothing escaped his eye or his mind. One who had had intimate and domestic contact with the Cardinal volunteered the information: "There was no question in the field of politics or religion that he could not answer with the competence of a scholar of vast culture and information."

Shortly before his death he was engaged in social studies relative to the origin of Bolshevism and Communism in

The Spiritual Life of Cardinal Merry del Val

various countries.

Michael Williams thus describes a visit he paid to the former Secretary of State of St. Pius X: "The Cardinal had consented to give guidance to the work in which I was engaged. 'Something about the problems of a journalist' I timidly said to the great Cardinal, who sat there watching me calmly and gravely, and listening with that courtesy and patience which everywhere mark the gentleman. I said that if he would speak to me as to the place that the lay writer could and should occupy in the modern movement of the Faith, I would treasure what he might say, and I would know that the paper I represented would have a trustworthy compass for its adventurous voyage. After a moment he spoke. He went on speaking for perhaps half an hour. This I may say, that as the Cardinal spoke I heard the Church itself speaking. There were great matters touched upon, even more than touched upon—emphasized and underscored. The subtle fire of irony, and the gleam of wit, and the charm of a conversationalist who conversed as a great artist might play his instrument, all this gave that half-hour's utterance a place forever set apart in my memories."[2]

The Cardinal was an orator of simple and facile speech. Whenever he gave an address at a religious gathering or a meeting of some social group, it was always really worth while. On May 21-22, 1922, he addressed the Fifth International Congress of Catholic Women's Leagues which was held at Rome. Here is a testimonial to his eloquence that appeared in one of the newspapers: "The address Cardinal Merry del Val delivered in French the day before yesterday

---

[2] *The Commonweal*—New York, March 19, 1930: pp. 549-550. Quotations from *The Commonweal* made with permission.

Portrait of a Man

created a very deep impression. The former Secretary of State to Pius X showed that he is both an orator and a thinker. We are not accustomed to hearing an address so rich in doctrine, so clear and logical in its presentation, so beautiful and elegant in style."

This significant testimonial finds support in what Princess Fanny Starhemburg wrote on August 22, 1932. As President of the Union of the Catholic Women of Austria, she referred to the Congress just mentioned, saying: "I shall never forget the address with which the Cardinal opened the Congress, an address of unsurpassing beauty both in style and in content. The principles developed by him at that time can undoubtedly be considered as a sure foundation for fruitful activity in the Catholic Women's movement all over the world."

As a diplomat, the Cardinal had a deep understanding of men and their passions as well as of contemporary movements in both the political and the religious fields. He believed that the Church by virtue of its faith was not just another society run in keeping with the ever-changing standards of human politics, but rather a society that lived and was conducted in accordance with supernatural principles, a society with a destiny clearly established for it by Christ.

Guided by justice in all his deliberations and judgments, he never failed to speak up for the truth even when others might have thought it advisable to remain silent or let it be taken for granted; even when others might have withdrawn from the controversy to protect themselves from biting tongues and sharp invective.

He never made use of arguments that could apply equally well to both sides of a question; opportunistic solutions were foreign to his make-up. He hated duplicity as

The Spiritual Life of Cardinal Merry del Val

much as he did an outright lie. One day someone remarked that the Lord will show great indulgence in judging liars because in certain lines of work it is not always possible to tell the truth. At this he became quite angry and indignant—indignation that was the natural reaction of a loyal and sincere soul.

He loved the truth, but the whole truth without any reservations whatsoever attached to it. It has been authoritatively testified that the things which meant most to him were honesty of character, rectitude of intention, duty, and the glory of God. The norm of his diplomacy was that of St. Pius X who once told a young prelate in the Secretariate of State: "You are young, but remember that politics in the Church consists in not playing politics but in always traveling along the right path."

The Cardinal was fully conscious of the fact that the Pope attached great importance and high value to whatever he said or advised. As a result, he felt the full impact of responsibility behind all his decisions. Before talking to the Pope, he would study and prepare; above all, he would pray.

One who was well acquainted with the religious and social life of Italian Catholics made this statement: "The diplomacy of the Cardinal Secretary of State was a natural product of his loyal and sincere character. He would not stand for subterfuge of any sort either in private conversations or in public affairs because to him the truth was always sacred. It was a diplomacy nourished with sentiments of justice and equity, sentiments that showed up even in his everyday associations, but were particularly evident in matters of great importance. It was a diplomacy interwoven with kindness and courtesy but foursquare with absolute firmness when the honor of the Church or the glory of the papacy demanded it."

This testimonial, however, should come as no great

Portrait of a Man

surprise since it is a known fact that Cardinal Merry del Val possessed on the one hand great virtue and on the other the rare gifts of prudence and ability—the two qualities that make up a true diplomat. A distinguished Roman prelate, thoroughly familiar with the Cardinal's diplomacy, said: "He combined a firm and upright character with sureness of tact that went right to the heart of the matter under discussion with the utmost prudence and extraordinary ability. He would not rush things; he knew how to wait it out and let time solve some of the problems. He possessed that calm and deliberate prudence which safeguards frankness of speech and freedom of action. He had the ability of knowing how to get around obstacles, of not letting difficulties disconcert him. Hence, matters of even a most delicate nature never found him unequal to the task."

It would be easy for us to furnish documentary proof of how the Cardinal's diplomacy reflected both prudence and ability. All one need do is go back and review the outstanding events in the pontificate of St. Pius X. But, since these qualities were deemed worthy of recognition and praise by the saintly Pontiff himself, we may limit ourselves to this statement by a French journalist: "The government of a state or empire is nothing in comparison with that of the Universal Church. After two conversations with Cardinal Merry del Val, I must confess that together with the memory of a most cordial reception I took away an impression and feeling of genuine admiration for the Secretary of State of Pius X. After the Holy Father he is the man to whom all Catholics owe a debt of gratitude and for whom they ought to pray."

This Cardinal who had spent the most fruitful years of his life in one of the most demanding positions in the

The Spiritual Life of Cardinal Merry del Val

Church had an extremely keen appreciation for all forms of art. His exquisite artistic taste was shown when he presided over the rearrangement of the Vatican Art Gallery and over the changes made in the apartments of the Pope and the Secretary of State.

But more significantly, he possessed an artistic inspiration which amounted to an instinct. He loved poetry, colors, and music. He had a beautiful voice and played the piano perfectly.

The Cardinal was an ardent devotee not only of music, but also of poetry and painting. He wrote several beautiful stanzas in English on Italy and sketched or painted in water color many different landscapes, especially those of Abruzzo.

During the last years of his life he delighted in photography. He took some really beautiful pictures in Italy, Switzerland, and England, always managing with the delicate touch of an artist to get the more subtle aspects of any landscape.

He was familiar with all the great musical masterpieces, especially Italian and German, and could recognize their composers after hearing the first few notes. He composed several sacred motets which were executed at various times in different churches of Rome and never failed to arouse admiration and favorable comment. St. Pius X took great pleasure in listening to the Cardinal give a perfect rendition of the Chant during services at St. Peter's.

In the spring of 1925, the Holy Father had consented to let the famous Polish pianist, Paderewski, hold a piano recital in his library. After the concert the Pope stayed awhile and chatted with those present. In the course of the conversation, pointing to the pianist Cardinal Merry del Val, he said in a loud voice: "Here is the Paderewski of the Sacred College!"

Portrait of a Man

At Subiaco or Monte Cassino, in the Umbrian valleys fraught with memories, amidst the Sabine Hills or the silent forests of the Alps, looking up at the rocky peaks with the blue background of the sky or at the perpetual snow, the Cardinal would spend hours contemplating the beauty and greatness of Almighty God.

During the last years of his life—from 1924 on—he used to go away during the summer for a short vacation to the quiet village of Arabba at the foot of the Dolomites. The morning of August 20, 1926—anniversary of the death of St. Pius X—he had climbed to the top of Mount Boe. It was over a thousand feet high and stood out from the plain a massive peak. Affected by the majesty of the awesome view, the Cardinal took off his hat and lifting up his beautiful voice intoned the "Gloria in excelsis Deo." An echo carried far and away the sound of his spontaneous and enthusiastic song of glory to the omnipotence of the Creator.

If Italy had been the Cardinal's native country he could not have loved it more. He visited all the fields of the great European War of 1914-18 and sought out the places where there had been fierce and bloody combat. He blessed cemeteries dotted with little white crosses on gentle slopes or under the shade of majestic fir trees. Once when climbing up the steep Colle di Lana, he stopped and gathered together unburied bones. He gave Christian burial to these heroic sons of Italy and over their graves planted the sign of the Resurrection and the Life.

When Cardinal Merry del Vel acted as Papal Legate to Assisi on October 4, 1926, he naturally was accorded every honor and consideration. In the twelfth-century drawing room of the historic Palazzo del Comune, he was made an honorary citizen of the renowned city of St. Francis. Paying homage to the leaders of his fatherland by adoption, he said:

The Spiritual Life of Cardinal Merry del Val

"I have lived in Italy for many years, almost my whole life, to the extent that I have acquired the right to call it my second fatherland." He loved it for its faith, for the classical tradition of its Roman-Christian culture, for the splendor of its art, for the musical quality of its language which he spoke perfectly, for its glories and misfortunes, its sacrifices and its tombs.

Cardinal Merry del Val was a man of deep and living faith who never forgot that he was a priest of God charged with administering the Divine Word that saves and redeems.

Apostle in Rome

"The years of my priestly ministry were the
most beautiful years of my life."
                CARDINAL MERRY DEL VAL

IV

Apostle in Rome

ST. Pius X had been a parish priest and a bishop whose one dominant passion was the salvation of souls, starting with his little parish in Tombola right up to the time he ascended the papal throne. The Lord gave him a Secretary of State who, from his earliest years, ardently longed to be a parish priest. He actually never experienced the joy of being a pastor but he certainly had the pastoral vocation and zeal, for from his first day in the priesthood until he died he lived for nothing but souls.

The Trinità dei Monti, the Cenacle, Villa Lante, Santa Ruffina, the Spanish College, San Silvestro in Capite, San Giorgio on the Piazza di Spagna were some of the many places in Rome where he heard confessions over the years or preached in the various European languages that he spoke to perfection. Whether he was in the confessional or in the pulpit, his charity, living faith, and extraordinary piety never failed to edify and provoke general admiration. God had bestowed upon him certain enviable gifts; a beautiful voice, expressive gestures, an easy and spontaneous flow of words, and a heart that was filled with love for Christ.

He possessed a deep understanding of spiritual needs and knew how to make his listeners start thinking; he could clarify their problems, persuade, and stir up their emotions. A man who heard him preach several times remarked that in him you could hear the "saintly priest full of love for God and of divine wisdom."

Immediately after his ordination to the priesthood, Raphael wanted to return to England and dedicate his life to convert work among the Anglicans, but Leo XIII kept him

The Spiritual Life of Cardinal Merry del Val

on in Rome as a member of the papal court. That was when God entrusted him with the souls of the children in the thickly populated section of Trastevere. That too was when God granted him a large measure of spiritual fatherhood, the most beautiful adornment of a priest.

While Merry del Val was still a student, a few days after having celebrated his First Mass, the President of the Accademia said that he had promised the principal of the Christian Brothers' School in Trastevere to send Raphael as spiritual moderator for the students. The promise was kept.

It must have seemed to the young priest that the Lord had finally heard his prayer. It was January 25, 1889, when he set out for Trastevere feeling like a native-born Roman and with all the enthusiasm of an apostle.

Here poverty seemed to walk the narrow streets and to glower from the broken-down houses and apartments that lined the alleyways. It was a far cry from the sort of life he had been accustomed to at court.

Monsignor Merry del Val saw immediately that no end of good could be accomplished in this world of boys. He set himself to work with all the enthusiasm he could muster. He was a youth among youth, and that was the secret of his success. He had everything necessary to captivate the hearts and souls of boys. In his handsome face there was a look of genuine serenity; there was tenderness in his eyes and pleasantness in his smile. He put up with the boys' frailties and was understanding. Nor did he lack that refinement of spirit to cure their spiritual weaknesses.

Accustomed as he was at all times to take a supernatural view of things, there was, however, one consideration that kept bothering him. What would happen to all these boys when the school year was over? He could visualize them being left to themselves. He wanted to save them from the misfortune of falling into temptations, to gather them all

Apostle in Rome

together into a small, compact group where charity and hope would safeguard their daily life. He dreamed of protecting them from evil and the viciousness of life, of educating them in virtue by means of an active program of prayer, work, and sacrifice.

So, after a year of prayer and preparation, on April 18, 1890, he founded the "Pious Association of the Sacred Heart of Jesus in Trastevere," which even today is one of the outstanding youth organizations in Rome.

His intention was to give the Church and society young men attuned to Christ, with strength of character and integrity, who would form the backbone of a solid Christian community. This was the goal he set, and nothing ever turned him from it.

At the outset there were some who thought the organization overstressed piety. Politely but firmly he said: "In the Association there shall be nothing but piety and love for Christ." Later, under the pretext of Catholic Action, some outsiders came and wanted to take over the meetings. This he prevented. At one time urgent requests were sent him through the mail to have the young men join in a mass meeting of protest against the insults leveled at Christ and the Church. He wrote this answer: "I am satisfied if I can turn out good Catholics and good family men; that way I am sure they will be excellent citizens. The Church of Christ puts its defense in prayer, in the love and charity of Christ, rather than in noisy demonstrations in public squares."

He never let himself be fooled or talked into anything. He was not interested in approval or disapproval, but in developing strong characters and flourishing Christian lives. He wanted robust piety, not noisy programs; purity of life, not worldly display. He was convinced that his boys, trained as they were in solid piety, would remember the wonderfully happy days they spent at the Association and

The Spiritual Life of Cardinal Merry del Val

that these memories would keep them from falling away from the Faith and all that is good and holy in life. He felt that, on occasion, they might even emulate that brave young Christian of long ago, St. Tarcisius who, though beaten and insulted, preserved the Blessed Sacrament from profanation.

All he wanted to do was win souls and offer them as a gift to the Lord. What did all the rest amount to? There in the midst of his boys, he was more than a spiritual director, he was a father who could understand their needs; a father who found pleasure in their childish and affectionate spirit of fun and who loved to take part in their games; a father who admonished them with tenderness and punished only when necessary, with a glance that weighed more heavily than the worst kind of reproof.

For forty years hardly a day went by without him spending some time with his dearly beloved boys. No duty, no honor, no assignment ever stopped him from visiting, at least for a few minutes, his charges in Trastevere. The day the news got out that he had been made a Cardinal and appointed Secretary of State his boys were overcome with joy but afraid at the same time that they might lose him. "No," said the Cardinal, "no, I shall never forget my boys of Trastevere." He kept his word. On the last Sunday of October in 1928, when celebrating both his feast day and the twenty-fifth anniversary of his elevation to the Cardinalate, he mentioned this, saying: "I have the comfort of knowing I have never gone back on my promise made twenty-five years ago."

This explains, too, a remark the Cardinal was in the habit of making: "Without seeing my boys, it seems as if I have not finished out my day." He would point to their snapshots and letters on the desk in his study, murmuring: "This way I seem to be right in the midst of them." He could talk that way and mean it because he truly loved his "Pious

Apostle in Rome

Association of the Sacred Heart of Jesus"; it was the apple of his eye, the light of his life.

Bishop Michael Gallagher of Detroit wrote as follows: "I was at Rome in 1929 and wanted to visit the Cardinal. I was told the place to find him in the afternoon was down with his boys at the Association of the Sacred Heart in Trastevere. And there I met His Eminence. He showed me the house with charming simplicity and told me what was being done for the boys. I found myself in the midst of a large number of boys who looked up at the Cardinal with filial reverence, their eyes beaming with pride that a Cardinal would deign to spend his spare time with them."

The First World War that broke the heart of his saintly Pontiff also robbed the Cardinal of many of his young men just when his work with them was reaching its peak, at a crucial phase in their spiritual formation. He bade farewell to the draftees with a smile on his face so as not to let them know the anguish he felt in his heart. He recommended them all to Christ, begging Him to watch over them during the war.

His help and encouragement followed them wherever they were, in the rear lines or trenches, on the fields of battle, in hospitals, or in prison. His great love for them manifested itself in every letter he sent urging them to do their duty courageously as Christians and soldiers for God and country.

When the war was over he had the comfort of gathering together those of his boys that were left, of greeting once more those brave young men whom he had seen leave and whom he had followed from afar, whom he had helped and safeguarded with his prayers.

The Association flourished anew, matured through duty fulfilled, firmer because of the trials undergone, wiser through suffering and sorrow, and with faith strengthened

The Spiritual Life of Cardinal Merry del Val

by the graces obtained when face to face with death.

The Cardinal saw his work spread through this thickly populated quarter of Rome like a mighty wave, renewing fervor and the practice of virtue. New generations and new families came along from boys whom he had started on their way. There could be no doubt about it now; he had molded good Catholics, good family men, and excellent citizens. In his heart the hope grew stronger with each passing day that all this good would not be dissipated with time, but, on the contrary, would grow progressively greater.

The last thoughts of his life, expressed in his will, were for the boys of his Association: "I bless my dear sons of the Trastevere"; and the last steps he took on that last evening of his life, February 24, 1930, were to visit his boys in Trastevere.

Two days later he was dead! But his boys did not forget him, and for five nights without a break, with tears in their eyes, they kept watch beside his body; they demanded they be given the honor of carrying his body to St. Peter's.

They certainly did not forget him and, on the first anniversary of the Cardinal's death, a memorial tablet was placed in the hall of the Association; it stands as a testimonial of their undying affection and sums up all the work he did as priest and educator.

Nor have his boys forgotten him over the years, for to this day the children of his old, original group in Trastevere take up the chant:

> Trastevere, Trastevere, be sure
> To keep remembrance bright and pure
> Of him whose visage, though austere,
> Was kindly, noble, and sincere,
> A brow that spells that he was wise
> And goodness shining from his eyes.

Apostle in Rome

The Cardinal never stopped hoping that some day might see the realization of that dream he had had al the outset of his priestly life—that England, the country of his birth, would become Catholic. The conversion of England was uppermost in all his thoughts. He never stopped praying for that intention. He always had his boys of Trastevere begin their meetings with a touching prayer to the Blessed Virgin, "For our brethren, the English," which he had helped compose.

Leo XIII wrote his famous apostolic letter to the English on April 14, 1895: "To the English who are seeking the kingdom of Christ in the unity of faith." In it he begged them to return to the Mother Church of Rome, and relying solely on the power of prayer, incorporated in it the Cardinal's prayer to the Blessed Virgin. It reflects the soul of a true priest and the heart of a real apostle. Here it is:

> O Blessed Virgin Mary, Mother of God, and our most gentle Queen and Mother, look down in mercy on England, thy Dowry, and upon all who greatly hope and trust in thee. By thee it was that Jesus, our Savior and our hope, was given unto the world, and He has given thee to us that we might hope still more.
>
> Plead for us, thy children, whom thou didst receive and accept at the foot of the cross, O Sorrowful Mother. Intercede for our separated brethren, that with us in the one true fold they may be united to the chief shepherd, the Vicar of thy Son. Pray for us all, dear Mother, that by faith fruitful in good works we may be counted worthy to see and praise God, together with thee in our heavenly home. Amen.

While yet a young Monsignor under Leo XIII, the Cardinal had worked zealously for the return of the

The Spiritual Life of Cardinal Merry del Val

dissidents in the land of his birth. He was deeply interested in the success of the Beda College in Rome. This college had been founded in order to give a solid Catholic education to those converts from Anglicanism who were aspiring to the priesthood so that they might then return to their native England as apostles of Christ.

Together with the saintly Father de Mandato of the Society of Jesus, he initiated the "Work for the Preservation of the Faith in Rome" to put a stop to an anti-Catholic movement, supported by Protestants in general and making use of all kinds of propaganda, which was at that time making itself felt in the very center of Catholicism.

But all this was not enough to satisfy the Cardinal's apostolic zeal. He felt that he had to go out into the Anglican world of Rome, enlighten it with his strong faith and robust doctrine, and lead it back along the sure paths of truth.

One who worked with him for ten years, from 1893 to 1903, in this new apostolate said that he seemed born to this kind of ministry: "Monsignor Merry del Val, a prelate of superior intelligence, profound humility, and enlightened piety, all charity and zeal, wanted nothing more than to shed light upon souls born in Protestantism and for the most part tormented by doubts. He had received from God exceptional gifts. His vast erudition and thorough knowledge of Sacred Scripture, together with his exquisitely courteous manner and humble dignity, succeeded in winning everyone's confidence. Hence, it was easy for him to convince them of their errors; to straighten out those who came to him for light and guidance."

Since he did not believe in hasty conversions, the Cardinal always proceeded slowly with those who came to him in search of the truth. He would instruct them patiently and carefully, convince them of their errors and prejudices, solve their difficulties, and remove all doubt from their

Apostle in Rome

minds. He would wisely and prudently allow them time to let the instruction fully mature; he wanted to be sure they were really prepared. He would weigh their thoughts, ideas, and sentiments, strengthen them in the Faith, and when the time came he would preside at the touching ceremony that ushered them into the fold of the true Church of Christ. One of his first converts was a seventy-four-year-old Englishwoman, who had been a Quaker for most of her life.

Moreover, the Cardinal never abandoned his converts or lost contact with them. Through correspondence or actual conversation he would follow them up, advising, helping, and encouraging them, but above all praying for them.

Certain proof of this lies in his voluminous correspondence, an eloquent testimonial in itself to his burning desire for souls. He had, as he himself pointed out, a consolation granted to very few indeed—he never had a single defection among his many converts. Another source of joy lay in the fact that many of his converts then became tireless apostles themselves in bringing the true light of Christ to those born and raised in Protestantism.

Death caught him still hard at work in convert-making: he died just as he was about to receive into the Church a soul from England. But the servant of God did not really discontinue his mission; he carried it on from above, for two years later that soul made her solemn abjuration of Anglicanism in the crypt of Westminster Cathedral.

"I am a Catholic," she wrote a day or so later to a lady of the Roman aristocracy, an intimate friend, "and have at last realized my desire of many years. When I received Communion for the first time, I had the feeling that the Cardinal, who took such great interest in me, was there near me, that he took me by the hand and accompanied me to the altar. The difficulties that stood in the way of my conversion and seemed insurmountable seemed to disappear almost like

The Spiritual Life of Cardinal Merry del Val

a miracle. . . . I have never been so happy in my life as I am now. I feel that the Cardinal is helping me and I am sure that he must be very happy about it up there in heaven."

Once again the Sacred Heart of Jesus had heard the plea of that touching "Prayer for a Soul," composed with all the mystic tenderness of a Psalm of David and so often recited by the saintly Cardinal. Here is his prayer for a sinner, to whom he tenderly refers as his "brother."

> Grant, O Lord, that the silent prayer incessantly rising before Thee, that the tears shed in silence, may intercede, O Heart of Jesus, for my brother who died.
>
> Died, but not bodily: his immortal soul died to the life of grace. Have mercy, Sweet Jesus, have mercy! May this soul not be lost forever.
>
> Oh, with what subtle snares the Tempter approached him with his fatal alluring deception! But my brother would not have died, O Lord, if I had been near him.
>
> But, alas! the pride of his spirit compelled Thee to move far away from him. He forgot; in fact, he scorned Thy advice: "Be ye meek and humble of heart."
>
> For the love Thy Mother had for him, hear this my prayer of anguish. Snatch him away from the Tempter's grasp. Save him, Lord, because he once loved Thee.
>
> Through the humiliations of Thy Passion, through Thy death on the cross, tell me, Lord, what Thou wantest of me—but give me that soul!
>
> Through the tender compassion of Thy Heart at the sight of human sorrow, let the heart pleading before Thee obtain favor, and may that soul now be won over by Thy mercy.
>
> Turn Thy glance toward him as Thou didst to Peter when he denied Thee. With that glance Thou couldst win him over because, Lord, he once loved Thee.
>
> Let us confess in his stead—he acted as a traitor. But

Apostle in Rome

perhaps some tender memory still lingers on in him. Reawaken it, O Lord, within his heart.

Heart of Jesus, Shepherd and Redeemer, Thou who dost save and redeem, have mercy on our wayward brother! Call out to him so that he may rise from his tomb.

Have mercy, Thou who hast never disdained the prayer of the sinner. Hear me too, O Lord, and call back to Thy Heart the wayward brother who has turned his back upon Thee.

Another field of apostolate and marvelous activity on the part of the Cardinal was, of course, St. Peter's Basilica where for sixteen years he held the office of Archpriest. No effort or care was ever too great for him; he spared no sacrifice to make this greatest temple of Christianity reflect the full measure of its magnificence and beauty.

The Vatican clergy greatly admired the Cardinal for his faithfulness in assisting at all the services in choir. If a Sacred Congregation or Papal Commission had a meeting scheduled for Sunday, he would ordinarily ask the Cardinal Prefect or President to excuse him from the meeting so as not to be absent from choir. Or if he had to arrange an appointment or a visit on some feast day, he always let it be understood that it would have to be after the Solemn Mass at St. Peter's.

When new members of the Chapter would go to pay him their respects, he invariably reminded them to be faithful to all the services in choir and when there to exhibit proper composure and dignity.

The Cardinal also had great concern for the sacred liturgy, for he looked on liturgy as a lesson that God teaches us. The execution of Gregorian Chant and other sacred music had to be in keeping at all times with the holiness of

The Spiritual Life of Cardinal Merry del Val

the house of God. He was keenly interested in the reform of sacred music and gave his full support to the work of the Association of St. Cecilia which encouraged the faithful to participate in the liturgical music of the Church. He contributed generously of his own money to the complete restoration of the five organs of the basilica. Likewise, for the convenience of the Vatican Chapter, he saw to it personally that a new edition was made of the Holy Week Office and the Offices for the Nativity of Our Lord and the Feast of the Apostles Peter and Paul.

The Cardinal loved the splendor and magnificence of the basilica. There were the tombs of Sixtus III and Julian II; a marble plaque containing the names of the 142 Sovereign Pontiffs buried within its walls. On its marble pavement were marked off the lengths of the great cathedrals of the world. Toward the end of his days the Cardinal showed his love for the basilica by having the pavement beneath the immense cupola done over in multi-colored marble. He paid for this with his own money, a lasting token of his deep attachment to the most wonderful temple in the whole world and of his constant devotion to the First Vicar of Christ.

The Cardinal gave to the basilica of the Prince of the Apostles his heart and mind, even his innate love for art. The final expression of his generosity was the gift of those things that were dearest to him—the gold chalice he had received from his family, the one he had used for over fort years to offer up the daily Sacrifice of the Mass.

Prayer and Penance

"It is up to us to turn our heart into a little Cenacle. Then nothing will upset us. There may be things to upset us on the outside but we can always find peace and recollection in the Cenacle of our heart."

CARDINAL MERRY DEL VAL

V

Prayer and Penance

The HEROES of history have a human greatness; in a saint, however, there exists a greatness far surpassing the merely human. There is, in a word, the divine element to be taken into consideration. It is not as easy to study this divine element as it is to consider the purely human aspect of a person's accomplishments, because holiness—the divine life within a soul—is a world reserved exclusively to the mysterious action of God. For this reason, perhaps, the best pages of the lives of the saints have never been written. Many manifestations of their heroic virtues will remain forever unknown, seen only by the eye of God.

In the case of the saintly Cardinal, all we can do is become partially acquainted with his interior life by studying what he said, wrote, or left us in his memoirs —a distant and faint reflection of the light that completely enveloped his soul.

There is this point to bear in mind: while his external life may not have been unusual, certainly his inner, supernatural life was most extraordinary. For whether he was wearing the simple garb of the priest or whether he walked in all the splendor and magnificence of the Cardinal, he was ever and always the "man of God," whose sole preoccupation was to translate into living terms that admonition of the Divine Master: "You therefore are to be perfect, even as your heavenly Father is perfect" (Matt. 5, 48).

Cardinal Merry del Val was truly a "man of God" for the simple reason that every day of his life he kept climbing the path of Christian perfection. He looked upon perfection as a living and active reality.

The Spiritual Life of Cardinal Merry del Val

He kept a little notebook of resolutions, and on one of its pages there is a statement which, without intending to do so, gives us some means of measuring the intensity of his spiritual life:

"By the grace of God I have promised: not to begin any action without reminding myself that He is interested in it; that He works with me and gives me the means to do it. Not to end an action without this same thought—offering it to Him as something which is His. During the action, whenever I remember, to stop a moment and renew my desire to please Him."

He never went back on this promise, for he lived with his eyes fixed on high, with his mind and heart lifted up to God.

The Cardinal composed a beautiful "Morning Offering to God Almighty" and would recite it daily before celebrating Holy Mass. We give here a shortened version:

My God, my Father and my All, the Beginning and the End of my existence; the most abject and wretched of all Thy creatures, I prostrate myself before the great throne of Thy ineffable Majesty; I worship Thee and bless Thee with all the faculties of my body and soul.

At the sight of my extreme nothingness I beseech the help of Thy merciful power, the assistance and protection of Mary, Thy Mother and mine, and that of all the angels and saints enjoying Thy presence, that I may be able to thank Thee in some way for the gifts and favors Thou hast deigned to grant me in Thy powerful goodness from the first moment of my existence to the present hour; for having seen fit to think of me, miserable worm of this earth, from all eternity; for having freely decreed my existence in preference to so many other possible things; and especially for having granted me another day in which to love and serve Thee.

I am on this earth for the sole purpose of serving Thee,

Prayer and Penance

O my God, and saving my soul.

I desire and firmly resolve today to use all created things in such a way and only in so far as they help me to attain my end.

Grant that my intellect, my memory, and my free will may be Thine forever.

I consecrate every beat of my heart, every breath, every word, and every movement of my soul and body to Thee, my God, with the sole desire of singing, with every faculty I have, a long hymn of praise to Thee, a hymn of expiation for my sins and of thanksgiving for Thy graces and benefits.

No one was better qualified than he to make the recommendation: "Every day give first place in your heart to the Lord. Never act with a view to please the world; let us have no human respect. Provided God is pleased, what does the rest matter?"

No one was certainly better able to write than he: "Do well whatever you do: do it for God and for God alone, and your life will be the first stanza of an everlasting canticle, the dawn of a happiness that will never have a sunset."

No one was ever in a better position than he to make the following observation: "Some outward successes may come your way, but what really counts is working solely for God, for His glory and the salvation of souls.

The interior life—the intimate communication of the soul with God—was a constant factor in the life of the Cardinal. He said as much himself a year after he had been made a Cardinal and Secretary of State, when writing to one under his spiritual guidance: "Pray the good Lord that if it be His holy will and His glory demands it I may be relieved of this assignment as soon as possible and be free to seek out along other ways my intimate union with Him."

In him faith took on the form of a living and profound

The Spiritual Life of Cardinal Merry del Val

prayer. All you had to do was see him, as his intimate friends not infrequently did, at prayer in his private chapel during those moments of deep recollection and intense concentration, with head slightly bowed and hands joined together and completely absorbed in meditation. You would have said that he felt and enjoyed an intimate union with God much in the manner of those contemplatives whom Dante Alighieri saw in the "Seventh Heaven" of his Paradise:

> The spirits of men contemplative, were all
> Enliven'd by that warmth, whose kindly force
> Gives birth to flowers and fruits of holiness.
> (Canto 22, 46-48)

We can readily understand, therefore, how he could honestly inculcate the following sentiments for the benefit of the souls he was guiding along the ways of Christian perfection:

"Our ordinary, everyday life should supply our interior life with constant nourishment. External things and circumstances should serve not to break down but rather build up the union of the soul with God and act as so many opportunities for virtue rather than for weakness or imperfection."

"In doing good," he added, "never seek applause from the world or approbation from men, but solely and exclusively God."

It comes as no great surprise that just before his appointment as Papal Chamberlain he wrote the following to his mother:

"I do not know what will happen to me or if I shall ever see realized my desire of working for the conversion of England.... But wherever I shall be, I hope to be able to do my duty for the greater glory of God." A hope, to be sure,

Prayer and Penance

that was not in vain; a promise that he never went back on, for all during his life his one goal was: "All for God and all for the glory of God!"

The Cardinal realized full well that the peak of detachment from oneself and from the things of the world consists in a ready and willing abandonment to God's holy will. Hence he used to advise his spiritual children: "Whether we like or dislike something is in itself unimportant. What counts is to know the will of God and on that basis make all our decisions."

"Once God's will is known to us, it becomes our path of duty and we should follow it with steadfastness and generosity of spirit."

And on another occasion: "It is up to us to accept with promptness and complete submission the dispositions of Providence, seeing in all things the will of God." Nor were these idle words or empty phrases, because if the Cardinal possessed a heart that loved God intensely, he had also a will that he sacrificed completely to God by making God's holy will the point of departure for all his thoughts and actions.

When he heard that the Pope had appointed him Papal Delegate in charge of the Extraordinary Mission to Canada, one of the first things Merry del Val did was to write the following letter to his dear friend in England, Monsignor Joseph Broadhead:

"You will have heard the news. The worst has happened, and I am to hurry off to Canada as Apostolic Delegate. I beg for prayers. It is only a temporary mission, but I fear it is the beginning of the end. God's will be done. The Holy Father has placed me under obedience and I go with a broken heart, but, I hope, determined to do God's will at any cost."

One well acquainted over the years with the soul and sentiments of the servant of God, summed up his memories

The Spiritual Life of Cardinal Merry del Val

in these words:

"Doing the will of God was, you might say, the life of his life. . . . He was always ready to accept any manifestation of the supreme will of God no matter what the cost in personal sacrifice.

"Rumor linked his name up with this Nunciature or that, especially after his return from Canada. The very thought of such an appointment made him very unhappy but he never prayed to be excused, fearful that he might be going counter to the will of God.

"Once when the rumor was very strong, and had him all but actually assigned to a certain Nunciature, I asked his permission to say some prayers begging the Lord not to let it happen. He agreed to it: but when I told him that he too should pray for this intention, he replied: 'No, I do not want to ask that for myself,' as if to say that he was ready to conform to the will of God."

Those in a position to know testify that he always remained the simple and humble priest who day by day went about doing the will of God even in the midst of all his work. Eloquent proof of this can be found in his "Morning Offering to Almighty God." In addition to that prayer, the Cardinal would start his busy day by saying:

"I am ready, O my God, to accept with complete indifference from Thy hands and in the way that may be most pleasing to Thee, health or sickness, riches or poverty, honor or dishonor, a long or a short life, friendship or hatred, always choosing only that which is in keeping with Thy glory. And if Thou art so good as to call me to imitate Thee more closely and intimately in poverty, in shame, and in suffering, here I am, ready and willing, dear Jesus."

This explains why whenever someone asked him about his health or how he felt, he would always smile and say: "The way God wants it." It also explains the particular

Prayer and Penance

emphasis he would give to the phrase of the Our Father "Thy will be done." According to those assisting at his daily Mass, whenever he came to those words, his voice would rise and become more resonant as if stirred into action by the prompting of his innermost being.

When the sad news was relayed to him that his dear mother was dying, the first words this serene and saintly man said were: "God's will be done!"

On another occasion when talking one day with a distinguished visitor about the salvation of souls, the Cardinal said: "The salvation of souls was my one burning desire and aspiration. I would have liked to dedicate my whole life to the apostolate of souls, but things were not disposed that way for me. The Lord's will be done."

So too, when a charitable lady, promoting a good work for destitute girls in Rome, came up against some obstacles and turned to him for advice, he told her: "Rely on Our Lord and go ahead with confidence as long as you can. God does not ask for more; success in what you do does not mean much. What really counts is doing what God wants, the way that He wants it done, and as long as He wants it done."

It is therefore understandable how, toward the end of his life, the Cardinal could write with a perfectly clear conscience: "How the years have flown by! I have been a priest for forty years, a bishop for twenty-eight, and a Cardinal for twenty-five. How different my life has been from what I had hoped and prayed for! God's will be done!"

God's will be done: the traditional aspiration of the saints. The Cardinal built around this thought a beautiful little prayer. It is as follows: "Most beloved Word of God, teach me to be generous, to serve Thee as Thou deservest, to give without counting the cost, to fight without thinking of my wounds, to labor without seeking rest, to spend myself without hoping for any reward except that of knowing that

The Spiritual Life of Cardinal Merry del Val

I do Thy will."

With his marked inclination toward the things of God, it stands to reason that the servant of God necessarily possessed, as already pointed out, both living faith and deep piety.

All who ever had the good fortune to assist at his Mass agree that during these sacred moments there was something supernatural about him. As one priest recalls: "If you never saw Cardinal Merry del Val celebrate Holy Mass, you really missed seeing something and would certainly be in no position to fully under stand him. The pronunciation of the liturgical words was clear and precise, and they were spoken with such unction as to convey even to persons of an irreligious frame of mind an understanding of the deep meaning behind the sacred texts.

Mrs. Ellin Craven Learned of New York wrote the following: "When Cardinal Merry del Val celebrated Holy Mass, his voice would be deep and vibrant: the movements of his hands expressed a feeling of indescribable adoration and faith."

The parish priest of Arabba, Don Angelo Frena recalling the trips the Cardinal used to make to this little town at the foot of the Dolomites during the summer months, states:

"The Cardinal would come to Arabba for a rest and for reasons of health. But the most important act of the day for him was always the celebration of Holy Mass. All his thoughts and affections, all the energy of this great soul seem to be concentrated on this divine Sacrifice.

"He always approached this sublime act with a heart all ablaze with faith; consequently, the way he celebrated Mass was a sermon, a silent but most eloquent one to be sure.

"That explains why all the good people of Arabba used to flock to his Mass and would leave the church remarking

Prayer and Penance

to one another: 'He is just like a saint!' "

A visitor from the United States, Mrs. S. W. Wood, was so struck by the extraordinary piety with which the Cardinal said Mass that she summed up her admiration and feeling by saying: "He seemed like another Christ."

Whether in the quiet of his private chapel or in the mystic silence of the Vatican crypt near the tomb of

St. Pius X, the Cardinal's faith and piety never failed to edify, to turn minds to thoughts of eternity, to touch

hearts and convert souls. What is more, the same result followed his appearances amidst all the splendor of the solemn functions at St. Peter's.

An old classmate from his seminary days at Ushaw in England, J. Scott of Los Angeles, California, wrote:

"I was in the Vatican Basilica on Holy Thursday, 1927, and saw the Cardinal placing the Blessed Sacrament in the Repository. From the expression on his face you could get some idea of the ardor of his faith and piety and I said to myself: 'This man is a saint!'"

Mrs. E. Craven Learned of New York, who had made up her mind to give up Protestantism, was in St. Peter's in 1927 during Holy Week. She watched the Cardinal during the solemn services on Holy Thursday, observing his profound recollection, even to the way he bowed and removed his zucchetto. She confessed that if a man of his intelligence could feel and show such deep faith, then indeed the Catholic religion had to have an undeniable foundation of truth.

On Ascension Thursday that same year, this lady assisted at Solemn Mass sung by the Cardinal and made the following entry in her diary: "All during the sacred ceremony I could see the Cardinal to whom I owed so much. More and more I was impressed by his manner, so quiet and composed, and his erect figure, never leaning ungracefully,

The Spiritual Life of Cardinal Merry del Val

as others do, but always straight, and, best of all, always recollected."

A Polish princess also made a similar remark in the course of conversation one day: "Only once did I see Cardinal Merry del Val praying at St. Peter's. But it is to him that I owe my return to the Catholic Church!"

It would certainly seem unnecessary to try to measure the extent of the Cardinal's love for God. Let it merely be said that his spirit of faith and piety was marked by that deep sensibility of which one often reads in the lives of the saints.

We have proof of this in the deep sorrow and pain his soul experienced upon hearing, even casually, any sort of blasphemy. At such times he became pale and the smile would die on his lips. One day he heard a cab driver viciously blaspheming the Blessed Virgin Mary. The Cardinal went up to him and rebuked him in a forceful but dignified manner. He then took down the number of the vehicle and told him he was going to report him as having violated the law. The cab driver was speechless with amazement: then he begged the Cardinal's pardon and promised that he would not use that sort of language again.

Another time, in a town outside of Rome, the Cardinal happened to pass by some workmen unloading bags of wheat from a truck. Because a bag had split open and was spilling some of the grain, one of the workmen started to curse like a man possessed, regardless of the fact that there were children standing near by.

The Cardinal was horrified but went on his way. For the rest of the day, however, he was greatly upset, and that evening besides his customary visit to the Blessed Sacrament, he made another one in reparation for the blasphemies he had heard. Such was his sensitiveness about honor for the Holy Name.

Prayer and Penance

The Cardinal had such great love for solitude and recollection that he avoided as much as possible all worldly affairs that might weaken his interior life. He put in an appearance only at those social gatherings where a wrong interpretation might have been placed on his absence. He did not like to attend society weddings; but he would readily go to those of his boys in Trastevere.

Whenever he left Rome for a few days of rest he preferred visiting those places where an atmosphere of silence and recollection prevailed—Subiaco with its sacred grotto; Assisi with its Franciscan sanctuaries; Orvieto where the Eucharistic miracle took place; Monte Cassino, Montevergine, the Valley of Pompeii, and many others.

A Private Chaplain of St. Pius X, Monsignor Giuseppe Pescini, who accompanied him quite often on these trips, made the following observation:

"If you accompanied the Cardinal on one of his pious pilgrimages, almost immediately you noticed in him a sudden transformation. It seemed he no longer saw or paid attention to anyone; he detached himself completely from everything about him to become absorbed in prayer."

The love the Cardinal bore the Poverello of Assisi is, of course, a fact that was well known. Many times he made a pious and devout pilgrimage to the Franciscan sanctuaries where the solitude was so conducive to colloquies with God.

His favorite sanctuary was Fonte Colombo—the hermitage so full of peace and silence where St. Francis had taken his two "most faithful followers" and dictated to them the Rule that was to govern members of his Order over the centuries.

The Cardinal used to go up there on foot in the afternoon, reciting the rosary with Monsignor Canali, stopping every now and then to admire the vast panorama

The Spiritual Life of Cardinal Merry del Val

of the valley of Rieti. Once he reached the sanctuary he never seemed to get enough of its mystic silence and spirit of recollection.

October 4, 1929, the last Franciscan feast celebrated by him on this earth, he wanted to devote entirely to the seraphic saint. He climbed up to Fonte Colombo in the morning to celebrate Holy Mass there and to distribute Communion to the members of the Community; then, like one unable to get enough of this place, he came back in the afternoon to be present at the impressive ceremony of the *Transito*. This is the name given by the Franciscans to a service they hold every year toward sunset on October 4. It commemorates the death *(transito)* of St. Francis; during the ceremony they sing Psalm 141, the same one the Poverello sang shortly before his death.

The Fathers tell us that the Cardinal arrived about an hour before the time set for the ceremony and went alone into the church. There, off in a corner, they discovered him on his knees, absorbed in prayer and utterly detached from the things of the world.

Then three days later he came back again, and this was his last visit.

The Cardinal heard the voice of God many times up there in the solitude of Fonte Colombo where the sight of the bleak rocks and dense forest lifted his soul in sublime meditation. We find proof of this in the Register for Visitors to the Hermitage. One day in the fall of 1923 he made the following entry:

"Today, October 10, 1923, upon completion of my fifty-eighth year of age, I pay a special tribute to the Poverello of Assisi: I thank God for having granted me all these years of life and I beg His pardon for not having served Him better as He deserved and as it was my duty to do."

Union with God

"Silence and recollection—prayer and activity—sacrifice and love."
CARDINAL MERRY DEL VAL

VI

Union with God

FOUR familiar devotions nourished the faith and piety of the Cardinal: devotion to the Holy Eucharist, to the crucifix, to the Sacred Heart of Jesus, and to the Blessed Virgin Mary. These were mystical sources from which he drew the strength necessary for his steady climb along the rugged road leading to God, the drive and vigor behind his spirituality.

Like all souls that have been given some insight into the secrets of the knowledge of God, he was keenly aware of the spiritual vitality hidden in the mystery of the Body and Blood of Christ.

"The Eucharist," writes Monsignor Cenci in his biography of the Cardinal, "was always, right up to his last moment, the center of his life, the flame of his heart, the light of his spirit."

We have already mentioned the "Morning Offering to Almighty God" which he composed and which he was accustomed to recite every morning before saying Mass. Here is another excerpt from it, highlighting his love for the Blessed Sacrament:

"I detest and weep for my past sins and negligences which, like a vast mountain, keep rising up before me.

"I weep for the sins and iniquities of the whole world, for the sacrileges and the indifference that we have shown Thee in the holy sacrament of Thy love.

I desire to make reparation and expiation for all these sins. I desire to live spiritually with Thee in the tabernacle, to visit Thee, worship Thee, and receive Thee spiritually wherever Thou art present under the sacramental veil and there live and die at the foot of Thy Eucharistic throne. Amen."

The Spiritual Life of Cardinal Merry del Val

During the day, at certain set hours, he would pray in his private chapel where the Blessed Sacrament was reserved—a privilege he always considered to be the greatest gift ever given him by St. Pius X—and there he seemed to be talking and listening to God.

He used to take personal care of the sanctuary lamp and saw to it that it was always burning. He never left the house nor returned to his room without first making a visit to the Blessed Sacrament. He invariably brought his busy day to a close with a visit to Our Lord in the Blessed Sacrament and would earnestly recommend this devotion to others:

"Make use of devotion to the Blessed Sacrament as a means of persevering in the practice of virtue. Let us go to Him toward evening and tell Him about our shortcomings, let us ask Him for help and forgiveness. Our Lord loves us, He thinks of us constantly, and His glance follows us every moment of the day."

The Cardinal used to carry the Blessed Sacrament in the Corpus Christi procession at St. Peter's and there, amidst all the splendor and magnificence of the solemn ceremony, one could really appreciate his deep faith and burning piety, his tender love and deep devotion to the Eucharist.

Mrs. E. Craven Learned of New York writes: "In these processions one saw the holiness and purity in the Cardinal's face, the expression of adoring faith and love, the beautiful eyes cast down or raised at times to look steadfastly at the monstrance, the lips moving in prayer. This remarkable expression of countenance came when adoring Our Lord, and could not be depicted in a photograph."

But the best testimonials of his ardent devotion to the Blessed Sacrament are, of course, his own thoughts and sentiments about Holy Communion; they are the expression, the heartbeat of an eminently Eucharistic soul. Here are just

Union with God

a few:

"When we receive Holy Communion, let us think of the greatness of the favor bestowed upon us. Our Lord gives Himself to each one of us as if there were no one else in the world outside of Him and us."

"During the day we should make frequent acts of spiritual communion so as to keep Our Lord constantly within us."

"Our best Communions are not those in which we seem to have a great feeling of tenderness toward Jesus in the Blessed Sacrament, but those in which we receive Him with greater humility, contrition, and confidence."

"Never deprive yourselves of Holy Communion because of discouragement. One of the tricks of the devil is that of making us exaggerate our shortcomings so as to keep us from going to Our Lord in the Blessed Sacrament."

"Let us remember that the best preparation for Communion does not consist in the recitation of set forms of prayer, often said with distraction or out of habit, but in the faithful fulfillment of our duties, accepting and offering to the Lord the troubles and opposition that come our way with the intention of making all these acts of ours serve as a preparation for Holy Communion."

"Let us live every day with the very life of Christ and ask Him to come to us on the last day of our life, to give Himself to us for the last time in Holy Viaticum, so that, holding us safely in His hands, he may lead us to the heavenly home of happiness and love."

Then there is the well-known Act of Spiritual Communion composed by the Cardinal in French. Later translated into many European languages, it had very widespread acceptance. The Sacred Congregation of Seminaries sent it to the spiritual directors of the regional seminaries of Italy with the recommendation "to avail

The Spiritual Life of Cardinal Merry del Val

themselves of the opportunity of distributing it to the students, to inculcate the deep Eucharistic piety which must be at the bottom of all their spiritual training." His Eminence wrote this prayer on July 14, 1902; the following is the English translation as it appears in the *Raccolta* (n.164b):

> At Thy feet, O my Jesus, I prostrate myself and I offer Thee the repentance of my contrite heart, which is humbled in its nothingness and in Thy holy presence. I adore Thee in the Sacrament of Thy love, the ineffable Eucharist. I desire to receive Thee into the poor dwelling that my heart offers Thee. While waiting for the happiness of sacramental Communion, I wish to possess Thee in spirit. Come to me, O my Jesus, since I, for my part, am coming to Thee! May Thy love embrace my whole being in life and in death. I believe in Thee, I hope in Thee, I love Thee. Amen.

In July of 1932 an Englishwoman by the name of Fraser Croft wrote to say that the daily recitation of this Act of Spiritual Communion had been a great source of comfort to her during an illness which prevented her from receiving Holy Communion; on December 12 of that same year, Catherine Mellor also wrote from England saying: "This prayer should be an inspiration to everyone and make us all strive toward that same ideal which the Cardinal had when he composed it and try to follow, at least in part, the wonderful example set by him in the love and service of God."

Whenever the Cardinal traveled outside of Rome, his first thought was to make a visit to the Blessed Sacrament on his arrival at the place where he was to stay. One day he happened to come into Poggio Fidoni, in the valley of Rieti. He immediately asked to see the pastor, a fine priest, and was told that he was away on a sick call. The Cardinal then

Union with God

expressed the desire of making a visit to the church. He went into the church and knelt down before the main altar to say some prayers. When he finished praying, he stood up and, glancing toward the tabernacle, noticed that it was only half closed. He mounted the steps of the altar, closed the tabernacle door, and locked it with the little key that had been left in the lock. Then he took a sheet of paper and wrote: "Would the pastor leave his safe wide open?" signing his name: "Cardinal Merry del Val." He took the tabernacle key, wrapped it in the piece of paper and left it on the altar.

Imagine the pastor's embarrassment when he got back and found the tabernacle key lying on the altar, and read the note with the Cardinal's signature!

The Cardinal could say with St. Paul: "For I determined not to know anything among you, except Jesus Christ and Him crucified" (1 Cor. 2,2), for every moment of his life he kept alive in his mind and heart the memory of Christ crucified. Ordinarily, the Passion of Our Lord was the object of his daily meditation and the theme he kept stressing in his sermons and in the many spiritual exercises he conducted.

He had a crucifix made of metal and richly indulgenced that he really treasured; he used to get down on his knees and pray before it every evening before going to bed, and at any other time when trouble beset him. Then too, he always wore a tiny cross, very old and very dear to him, hanging about his neck night and day.

He read over and over again a little book written in French and entitled: *Elevations on the Sorrows and Teachings of the Sacred Heart of Jesus during His Passion.* He used to distribute it among his pious friends, urging them to cultivate devotion to the Passion of Christ. Among other books he advised reading, he would single out *The Passion of*

The Spiritual Life of Cardinal Merry del Val

Our Lord Jesus Christ by the famous Father Bourdaloue.

The Cardinal left many spiritual letters and ascetical notes written under various circumstances in both prose and poetry; there we find many thoughts that reflect the ardor of his piety and the deep devotion he always had for the crucifix:

> Have a great devotion to the Passion of Our Lord, and, mindful of the love that He has shown for us, let suffering open up your heart just as it opened up His.
>
> Our Lord was not content with giving us only a part of Himself, but gave us all of His Blood. Learn to be generous toward Him, not to measure your sacrifices. Do not be satisfied with doing only that which is strictly necessary for your salvation, but give Him with generosity whatever He asks of you.
>
> Put yourselves before Christ on Calvary. Look at what He has done for you and what you have done for Him. See the difference, and you will realize how much love you ought to have for Him.
>
> With peace and resignation put up with your daily troubles and worries. Remember that you are not disciples of Christ unless you partake of His sufferings and are associated with His Passion.
>
> Consider yourselves fortunate indeed if Our Lord, who has loved you so much and suffered so much to prove His love, gives you an occasional opportunity to suffer a little for Him and thus prove your love for Him. Be glad to pick up the thorns you encounter on your journey and make them into a crown.
>
> Let us learn to love the cross, to accept it as our heritage, as the norm of our life, and to bear it in silence because the help of the grace of silence was the only thing that enabled the saints to carry their extremely heavy crosses.
>
> Let us accept crosses with resignation and love: the

Union with God

crosses of everyday life, interior crosses, crosses of the moment at hand. Our Lord showed His love for us by carrying the cross: we too can show our love for Him by accepting with joy the cross He sends our way.

Such are the sentiments of a man whose lips and pen always seemed inspired by the idea of silent suffering and hidden sacrifice. Shortly before he died he wrote as follows: "By His Passion Christ wanted to teach us the value of suffering; by what He went through He merited for us patience to put up with our afflictions. Let us love suffering, or at least accept it out of love for Him who sends it to us with so much love, like a treasure with which to win everlasting happiness. We must never forget that one way of pleasing the Blessed Virgin Mary is to meditate and contemplate Her Son Jesus suffering on the cross."

This was certainly the dominant passion of the great prince of the Church. One day, with the vision of the cross before his eyes, he made this entry in his spiritual diary: "Silence and solitude are the atmosphere of the cross, and secrecy is its natural climate. The cross is a gift the Lord makes to those whom He loves."

Thus did the heart of Merry del Val react in the dark hours of misunderstanding, of bitterness and opposition. Amidst the confusion of ideas and the conflict of human passions, he would go to the feet of his Master and make a holocaust of his worries and troubles. When trials and suffering came his way, he would steadfastly remind himself: "In my troubles and tribulations I shall think only of Christ on the cross, completely abandoned and despised by all." His soul would rise to the occasion with the heroic resolution: "I will offer myself up constantly, ready and willing to suffer much for the love of Christ and for the Church, even to a point of dying for Jesus who died for love

The Spiritual Life of Cardinal Merry del Val

of me"—words that sound like a distant echo of those spoken to him by St. Pius X when exhorting him to accept the cross of Secretary of State: "We will work together and suffer together for love of the Church."

Devotion to the Sacred Heart of Jesus was one of the outstanding characteristics of the servant of God. When he was a boy he enrolled in the "Apostleship of Prayer," the confraternity of devotion to the Sacred Heart of Jesus. Every month he received the leaflet from the National Director in England. The last one arrived after his death. It had been mailed from London on February 25, 1930, the day before he died.

As he grew up, this tender and consoling devotion developed within him and became more fervent, more intense and profound. We have conclusive evidence of this in the "Pious Association of the Sacred Heart" which he founded in the thickly populated section of Trastevere. The inspiration behind the foundation had a threefold supernatural goal: "To render unto Christ love for love. To imitate the virtues taught and practiced by the Divine Master during His life on earth. To make reparation and expiation, with every possible means, for the sins of mankind, especially for those committed against Our Blessed Lord in the Holy Eucharist."

Hence, every Sunday before Benediction of the Most Blessed Sacrament and at all their meetings it was customary for the boys to recite in common the Litany of the Sacred Heart of Jesus. It was always edifying to see the Cardinal devoutly praying with them before a beautiful picture of the Sacred Heart of Jesus. This picture, incidentally, had been painted especially for the Association and was in keeping with the ideas suggested by the Cardinal. It was just as edifying to see him, without fail,

Union with God

every Friday down among his boys in Trastevere and hear him talking to them about the Sacred Heart. Edifying too was the way his face would light up with joy every time he heard his boys sing in unison the touching invocation: O Heart of boundless love, now and ever take pity on us."

Tireless promoter of devotion to the Sacred Heart of Jesus, no sooner had he been named President of the Accademia dei Nobili Ecclesiastici when he introduced among the students the First Friday devotions. Moreover, he made it a point to be on hand punctually for these pious exercises.

In daily conversation, in spiritual guidance, in the many sermons and conferences he gave religious communities, first as prelate, then as bishop, and later as Cardinal, his one dominant thought was the Divine Heart of Jesus as a powerful means of sanctification, an infinite fountain of mercy, and a sure anchor of salvation.

He was very happy to be named Cardinal Protector for the Society of the Sacred Heart founded by St. Madeleine Sophie Barat. Every time he visited a new house of this Society, his greeting would always be: "With all my heart do I bless this new house so that it may become another hearth of love for Our Blessed Lord."

"Devotion to the Sacred Heart of Jesus. Live at the school of the Sacred Heart: study and imitate It, work and suffer for the Sacred Heart!" Such was the program set up for himself by the servant of God in December, 1899, shortly after being appointed President of the Accademia. It was a program he lived up to for the rest of his life.

"Be brave! From the Heart of Jesus comes grace, strength, and help!" This was his word of command and he never fell short of it. His favorite aspiration, one that seemed to grow stronger instead of weaker with the passing years and changing circumstances, was the prayer he himself

The Spiritual Life of Cardinal Merry del Val

composed:

"O most sweet Jesus, my joy, my hope, my All, open Thy Sacred Heart to me and reveal to me its allurements. Unite me to It forever. Grant that all the aspirations and all the movements of my heart, which cease not even during sleep, may be a proof of my love for Thee, and may they say to Thee: 'Yes, Lord, I am all Thine.'

"Yes, O Jesus, I wish to seek out, as Thou didst, a crown of thorns with which to love Thy Most Sacred Heart."

For Cardinal Merry del Val devotion to the Blessed Virgin Mary meant getting closer and closer to Christ by knowing and loving Him better with each passing day. Time and again he would say: "Have great devotion to the Blessed Virgin because the more you have of it, the closer you will get to Our Blessed Lord. It is impossible to have devotion to the Blessed Virgin without loving Our Lord more."

One of his more frequent aspirations was the following:

"O Mary, my Mother, how I love thee! Thou teachest me all that I have to know and all that really matters to me, for thou teachest me what Jesus is for me and what I ought to be for Him."

His tender devotion to Mary, the Mother of God, grew stronger with the passing of time, and when he was fully matured it developed into an undying flame. When he was a young Monsignor at the court of Leo XIII, then later President of the Accademia and Archbishop of Nicaea, he never missed attending the pious exercises in honor of Mary conducted in Trastevere. A few survivors of the original group—today well up in years—still reverently recall some of his tender sayings about the Mother of God. He knew how to enkindle or reawaken in their hearts love and devotion to the Blessed Virgin. They still remember that extraordinary piety with which he instilled in them devotion

Union with God

to the holy rosary, especially during the month of May.

He used to tell the boys: "When we feel weary of life and all its problems, let us pick up the rosary and meditate upon the Joyful Mysteries, considering the family life of Jesus Christ and how He lived it.

"When all we seem to want are pleasures, let us recite the rosary, meditating upon the Sorrowful Mysteries.

"When we feel we have become overly attached to the things of this world, let us recite the rosary, meditating upon the Glorious Mysteries."

The Cardinal was deeply devoted to making Mary known and loved. His own thoughts and sentiments are the best proof of this. Here are some of them:

"After having given us everything else, Our Blessed Lord wanted to give us His own Mother. Let us, therefore, turn to Mary every day with humble confidence and beg her to grant us the grace of being faithful until death."

"Be closely united to Mary. Make your Communions one with those of the Mother of God. In your prayers, in your sacrifices, in your troubles and in all of your actions, stay close to her. Then your spiritual life will rest upon a solid foundation."

"Mary carried Our Blessed Lord to St. John the Baptist on her visit to St. Elizabeth, so too should you try to carry Christ to those near you. Try to make the Blessed Virgin known and loved and do not be discouraged by the thought that perhaps you are not worthy. The Lord sometimes makes use of the most inept and lowly instruments."

He loved the sweet Mother of God. He often talked about her and would write about her rather with his heart than with his pen. When created a Cardinal, he entrusted to Mary his whole future as a prince of the Church. When named Archpriest to the Vatican Basilica, he again showed his love and devotion for the Mother of God by making the Feast of

The Spiritual Life of Cardinal Merry del Val

the Purification (February 2, 1914) the date for the ceremony of his investiture.

His daily recitation of the rosary and the many pilgrimages he made to the various sanctuaries of the Blessed Mother—practically the only respite he took from his work—speak more eloquently than words of his undying love for the all-beautiful, all-pure, and all-holy Virgin Mother of God. The sanctuaries of Mary at Loreto, at Gennazzano, in the Valley of Pompeii, at Montevergine, the famous one at Einsiedeln, and even the little sanctuary of the Madonna at Cendrole in Riese, so dear to the heart of St. Pius X, all saw him kneeling before their altars, murmuring the prayer which he himself had composed:

"O Mary, my sweet Mother, great is my love for thee, and yet it is all too little! Thou teachest me what I needs must know, for thou teachest me what Jesus is to me and what I ought to be to Jesus. Mother well-beloved, how near must thou be to God, and how completely art thou filled with God! In proportion as we know God, we are mindful of thee. Mother of God, obtain for me that I may love Jesus; obtain for me that I may love thee."

There are not many, however, who know about his special devotion to the Mother of Sorrows. Few are aware that under his prelate's robes he wore the badge of the Third Order of the Servants of Mary; that day by day he lived in keeping with the spirit of that Order. Moreover, when talking in private about the sorrows of the Blessed Virgin, his conversation always became more animated. In offering solace and comfort he never failed to leave souls with the thought of the sorrows of Our Blessed Lady. He wrote the following on September 16, 1903, when he was Pro-Secretary of State:

"For me the Feast of the Sorrowful Virgin is the most beautiful of all the feasts of the Madonna because it

Union with God

commemorates the great sacrifice of our Mother, in which we find a summary of all her virtues. Sorrowful, yes, but ever beautiful, ever grand, ever immaculate:

'I am black, but beautiful.' Serene in her martyrdom, like a true handmaid of the Lord: how intense was her love for us! Let us offer up everything to the Heart of Jesus through the hands of the Sorrowful Virgin.

"Be brave! Look at the cross and then look at the foot of the cross where the Blessed Virgin Mary,

Mother of God, stands overwhelmed with bitter sorrow. Unite your troubles and afflictions with hers and consider how much she suffered."

Then in another letter he returned to the same topic: "Your place during these days of Holy Week should be at the foot of the cross of Christ on Calvary, next to the Virgin Mary. If the darkness surrounding you prevents you from seeing Christ, reflect that even the Blessed Virgin could then no longer see Christ. Nevertheless, she remained by His side at the foot of the cross."

Shortly before his death, he expressed this thought:

"Do not look on consolations as a goal in themselves, but accept them as a means granted by God in order to strengthen us. Do not let crosses become an obstacle, but sanctify them through resignation and offer them up to the Lord. Let us ask the Blessed Virgin Mary, Queen of Martyrs, to help us. She it was who spoke the *fiat* to all suffering and sorrow."

Here we might add that the Cardinal, from the time he was a Papal Chamberlain, had entrusted to the Sorrowful Virgin the return to Holy Mother Church of his separated brethren in England. Every evening he recited the Rosary of the Seven Dolors of Mary and during the night kept the rosary entwined about his right arm as a token of his tender love for the Virgin Mary. Then, too, among the many

The Spiritual Life of Cardinal Merry del Val

pictures he kept in his bedroom first place was reserved for the beautiful image of the Sorrowful Mother—a copy of the one venerated in the Basilica of Santa Maria in Trastevere.

When Secretary of the Sacred Congregation of the Holy Office, the Cardinal bought a plaque of the Virgin and had it put up in the vestibule of the building. In addition to his tender devotion, he also used his artistic mind to honor Our Lady. He conceived the idea of a picture which he called the "Desolata," and had it painted for the altar in his private chapel. It is a touching picture. The Mother of God stands upright, with hands joined together and completely overwhelmed with her sorrow, looking down on a table on which are lying the scourges, the crown of thorns, and the nails that were used to torment her beloved Jesus. The tears in her eyes, the pallor of her countenance, her general attitude of utter abandonment bring out forcefully the extreme cruelty of her suffering and sorrows, and the heroic patience of her soul. In suggesting these devout features to the painter, the Cardinal had, without realizing it, revealed the extent of his own devotion and shown how well he understood the sorrows of Mary.

The Director of Souls

"All for God! Let our work, our actions and our sufferings be for Him alone; let our soul and our body, now and ever, bow down in generous submission to His holy will."
CARDINAL MERRY DEL VAL

VII

The Director of Souls

PRIEST whose gaze was always centered on the supernatural, Cardinal Merry del Val guided souls with a sure hand and kept them in a high spiritual atmosphere such as he himself lived in. Consequently, as a spiritual director there have been few like him. Mrs. Montgomery of London, who knew him personally, says: 'His experience in the direction of souls was so well known and appreciated that even non-Catholics came to him for advice."

The Cardinal's spiritual direction left a deep impression on souls, because it was above all firm yet gentle, precise yet full of feeling. He never got lost in mere theories or empty formulas. With a few well-chosen words he would point out the right road to follow and would inspire a soul with courage and strength. There seemed to be a supernatural air about him that won people over completely. He understood souls intuitively and evaluated them in relationship to God, taking into account their bright and dark sides, their troubles and difficulties, and he would pray for them. He had acquired the difficult art of listening with the utmost attention and always showed such kindness that souls would lay bare all their secrets with trust and confidence.

One of his penitents, a certain Marquis Misciatelli, had this to say: "In the direction of souls he acted like a kind father. It seemed as if he was able to read the problems of a soul, for more than once that sort of experience happened to me.

"He was full of compassion, but demanded obedience: once he expressed an opinion or gave advice after mature

The Spiritual Life of Cardinal Merry del Val

reflection, he never backed down or changed his stand.

"He insisted, above all, upon absolute trust and filial confidence. He would tolerate no misgivings because, he used to say, they only come from lack of trust in God.

"He would say: 'It is not necessary to recite a lot of prayers, but it is necessary to pray with fervor, to pray well.' Hence, he always recommended a short recollection before prayer, putting oneself in the presence of God; and if there was not enough time, he preferred that you shorten the prayer rather than omit this preparation.

"A single word from him was enough to bring peace to the soul: it would dissipate any anxiety or agitation and put an end to any fear. He always concluded with a thought on Our Lord's love for us: one of his favorite sayings was: 'Jesus loves you with a love the tenderness of which you will never be able to understand.'

"One might say that when he spoke to you, you heard the voice of Christ."

Another penitent wrote: "His teaching revolved constantly about this point: 'Strive for holiness within your own state in life. Be at peace wherever God has put you and do His holy will.'

"He was deeply interested in one's family affairs, career, material problems, and health.

"His penitents could visit him at any hour of the day because he never bothered about his own inconvenience or personal sacrifice.

"The souls under his spiritual guidance were constantly in his thoughts: he remembered them in his prayers and he always had some paternal advice or wise counsel to give them."

One of the Cardinal's penitents was a distinguished foreigner who had spent practically his whole life in Rome. These are his impressions: "Despite his many occupations

The Director of Souls

the Cardinal's time was always at the disposal of his penitents. You could go to him even when he was Cardinal Secretary of State without any fear of inconveniencing him because, for him, souls were the only thing that counted.

"Since he himself was extremely pious he wanted us to give God the best we had in us: all the rest was secondary.

"He used to say: 'When you reach the point in your spiritual life where there is no longer any enthusiasm or pleasure, that is when you start working solely for the Lord and when real merit begins.'"

One of the English Sisters of the Little Company of Mary writes thus: "As spiritual director he knew how to inspire souls with the same wonderful ideal of holiness that he himself had. He used to say: 'First do the ordinary things well, then you can think of extraordinary things.'"

The Cardinal was overburdened with so many duties and grave responsibilities in the service of the Church that he never found time to write a formal work on ascetical theology. All that he left in writing were some sketches of meditations, a few sermon outlines, some thoughts and reflections, and his concise letters to those who sought his spiritual direction.

These letters, from some of which we shall quote, show how his spiritual teaching on the sanctification of souls hinged on one basic idea—accepting the will of God with love and confidence.

Here is an example from a letter he wrote to a prominent lady in Rome: "You tell me you are very ill and do not have enough strength to perform your customary pious exercises. This is the same as saying that you are living the life of a sick person. But if you live that life in the true spirit of conforming to the will of God, you have within your grasp a wonderful means of sanctification, because then your

The Spiritual Life of Cardinal Merry del Val

whole life becomes a continuous act of piety. So, forget all about these apprehensions of yours and go ahead day by day and our by hour and leave everything to the good Lord who is at work within your soul. Be brave; I do not forget you at the altar."

On October 27, 1929, four months before he died, he wrote another letter to the same woman: "You have received a great deal from the Lord and now you have to show your gratitude by living a more fervent religious life, one that is calm, positive, and fruitful, by trying to do the will of God at all times. Often turn to Our Lord and say: 'Let whatever pleases Thee, please me; let it be my passion and my love. Let me be totally indifferent to whatever happens; let me love whatever is Thine, but let me love Thee above all, my God.'" The Cardinal taught sanctification through sacrifice, the cross, and suffering, but he never abandoned a soul in time of trial. On September 16, 1903, when Pro-Secretary of State, he wrote to one of his penitents:

"I do not forget you in my prayers during these days of your great trial. I have asked the Lord to bless you in a special way. Then on Sunday I shall say Mass for all your intentions. I am sure you must have suffered during these days and that your loyalty to Jesus must have been put to the test. Let the storm roll on its way: love the cross. Offer up everything to the Heart of Jesus through the hands of the Sorrowful Virgin who by her fiat accepted all the suffering and sorrow that were to be hers.

On March 1, 1912, he wrote: "I never forget you in my prayers and follow all your steps. No doubt about it, the Lord is sending you a cross, and that is the way it has to be; as a matter of fact, you ought to be content with it because it supplies you with the material that you need to build and prepare your throne in paradise and it lets you go deeper and deeper into the sanctuary of the Most Sacred Heart of

The Director of Souls

Jesus."

On January 8, 1923, he wrote to another afflicted person: "Your life has often been saddened by darkness and obscurity but the Lord has never abandoned you in the midst of your trial, as you probably understand now and will understand even better in the future. The cross has served the purpose of purifying your heart.

"O blessed obscurity that has been the source of so much light! The experience you have had should be a source of strength to you, helping you to always make use of such trials to rise above any earthly affection and strengthen your union with God."

And again on April 24, 1925:

"I am very sorry that you are sick again and I can certainly appreciate how much you have to suffer, even morally. Take up the cross which the Lord gives you; not as if it were your cross, but His cross, a portion of which He offers you. Through love and joyful acceptance make it become yours.

"In the meantime also pray for me: I need prayers at this moment for I have just received the sad news that my mother is about to leave this earth. God's will be done!"

It might be noted here that the Cardinal's mother died seven days after he had written this letter.

Such was the goodness of his sensitive heart that when souls came to him with their troubles, fears, and uncertainties, he would go out of his way to offer consolation and encouragement.

"Your letter reached me yesterday," he wrote one day. "I have read it and reread it carefully and have given much consideration to all that you told me in confidence.

"I have asked the Lord for help, and it is not hard for me to give an answer because I have a clear picture of what I have to say. Accept your trial willingly, shut your eyes and

The Spiritual Life of Cardinal Merry del Val

go ahead, from moment to moment, trusting in the mercy of the Lord, without looking ahead and without questioning anything. Your virtue will, as a result, be much more solid and meritorious than it would be in moments of comfort. Let Jesus work in your soul in whatever way He desires, while you remain at His feet, resigned and satisfied with just being useless."

In the case of one about to make a decision in the matter of her vocation, he suggested that the following be kept in mind:

"I understand perfectly how this last phase of the sacrifice you are about to make can be very painful and I suffer together with you. But there is a Calvary: upon this Calvary you suffer without any human consolations, but at the same time you love with pure and supernatural love, a prelude to the ineffable joy we shall have in our everlasting union with God. Look at the Blessed Virgin at the foot of the cross, and you will understand this even better. Suffering itself passes, but the fact of having suffered remains forever.

"Be brave! Any soul consecrating itself to God must pass through a test such as this that purifies and forges the heart, because the more one gives the more one suffers. But Our Blessed Lord is always there beside us and He invites us to confide in Him our sufferings and tribulations.

"I pray for you every day, and ask you to remember me in your prayers."

In answer to a woman who complained because poor health compelled her to lead a life of forced inactivity, he said:

"I rejoice with you. What could possibly be more useful to the soul than for the Lord to permit sickness to prevent us from following the normal course of our activities; that is a great grace and privilege He bestows upon us. To live more intimately with God and for the love of God, to increase

The Director of Souls

your spirit of prayer and of self-mortification, to renounce from hour to hour external satisfactions and the distractions of your senses is an ineffable joy, a dynamic peace, an apostolate that will help souls. By living this way we can be sure we are not placing obstacles in the way of God's action in us and in others because of an external activity which is often full of self-love and animated by human motives. I bless you with all my heart and bless all of your intentions."

Sometimes he seemed almost intuitively to put his finger right on the many perplexing problems and worries that often afflict souls trying to make some real progress in Christian perfection. With a few firm and sure words he knew how to restore peace and calm.

"Don't think even for a moment," he wrote in 1916, "that you should cut down on the frequency of your Holy Communions: on the contrary, the more you seem to suffer, the darker things get and the more afflicted you are, the more you ought to seek relief at the fountain-head of the Eucharist where Jesus waits for you every day, even though He may be hidden and silent. Please believe me when I say that the trial you are going through now contributes to your sanctification and is of utmost benefit to your soul; it is an occasion of merit and a pledge of love. Be of good cheer. If the Lord calls you to struggle along in aridity and with but few comforts or consolations, it is a sign that He considers you capable of facing up to your trial and He will certainly give you the strength to put up with it."

He wrote on June 25, 1917:

"I may be perhaps indiscreet, but reading your letter I feel I want to tell you something.

"This morning in chapel I watched the little light burning before the Blessed Sacrament and saw the wick that sometimes smokes, crackles, or blazes up, but always goes right on burning and is consumed almost without shedding

The Spiritual Life of Cardinal Merry del Val

any light. No one pays much attention to it, and for many hours nobody even looks at it; it suffers by comparison with the more beautiful candles, the bright flowers, the gold candelabra or the precious vessels. Yet, no one would ever think of saying that it is useless. After all, you cannot get along without the 'wick' as it goes on fulfilling its modest mission faithfully and constantly. It symbolizes a love that has its faults, to be sure, but one that remains loyal and true. There is nothing striking about it but it is more pleasing to the Lord than other more showy and highly admired gifts that are offered to Him.

"Jesus looks at our hearts and knows how to evaluate our dispositions, just as He knows how to sympathize with our shortcomings and reward our modest efforts of good will. I bless you with all my heart."

From another letter written on September 29, 1926, we get this comforting thought:

"It is not good to become dejected at the sight of your faults and frailties: the consciousness of our sins and the sight of our shortcomings is a grace of the Lord that saves us from so many illusions. Let us leave it up to Christ to see the good and let us rejoice in our humiliations and in the awareness of our nothingness; let us work in the field where He wants us to be, without being concerned about the harvest that is being reaped, for it is better that we know nothing about it. Be of good cheer and have confidence in the Lord's infinite goodness. I bless you with all my heart."

The Cardinal was not in favor of taking time out for rest in the march toward perfection but demanded constant progress. If someone started to lag behind, he would point this out to him in no uncertain terms, as shown in a letter dated July 24, 1898:

"I am aware that you are still the victim of what threatens to become a chronic disposition to lose courage.

The Director of Souls

You have to fight this tendency with all your might. It is an ugly fault and hard to reconcile with true humility which is the same as saying that it is hardly compatible with genuine virtue.

"Success is a dangerous thing for the majority of souls because very few are able to bear its weight, and in your case it is a very dangerous thing. Your desire to succeed should extend no further than willingness to do the best possible in the eyes of God. When you have done this, you will have attained success. But if failure should result, at least externally, then thank the Lord for protecting you from pride which in all probability would have overtaken you if you had acted from merely human motives or with the idea of taking pleasure out of your successful venture. Scrutinize your acts of thanksgiving after an external failure, especially if this failure is accompanied by a burning desire on your part to seek your own happiness.

"I do not want to leave you standing idle with arms folded; you have to keep going ahead and, when you do not succeed, be glad and thank God who is keeping everything safe for eternity."

On October 27, 1916, he wrote:

"How do you intend to get to paradise and to Our Blessed Lord—with roses? But surely you don't see them around His head or around His heart. Just what sort of material would you like to work with? With nice and pleasant things, possibly, that do not offend your sensitive nature? What kind of stairs do you intend to use to climb up to heaven? Could it be stairs without steps?"

Because the Cardinal loved souls in God and because of love for God, he always showed concern for the many problems and worries that go with family life, and the grief that often accompanies the bond of human affection.

On May 13, 1916, he wrote:

The Spiritual Life of Cardinal Merry del Val

"I would like to see in you a gentler spirit of resignation in your genuine sorrow. Do not merely aim at suppressing your grief but try to sanctify it gently with Our Savior. You have a treasure right in your hands enabling you to practice virtue in an eminent degree: do not waste it. Your grief is legitimate but offer up everything tenderly to Christ and ask Him to be your comfort. Accept the sacrifice and do not let yourself be overcome by grief by constantly recalling it to mind. I send you my blessing and remember you in my prayers.

In 1921 he wrote to one of his spiritual daughters, who was praying hard for the conversion of her husband, and gave her these words of comfort:

"I continue to pray for you every day and I ardently desire to see your husband obtain the light and grace to enter the Catholic Church."

And in another letter, written to her in 1924, he concludes:

"I shall continue to pray fervently that he may also receive that other grace which would put the crowning touch to our happiness."

Then, writing to one who had lost her mother, he gave these thoughts on sacrifice and resignation:

"Do I have to tell you that I partake of your grief and never stop thinking about you and praying to the Lord that He may sustain you at this sorrowful time?

Under the heavy burden of your heartache, you tell me that you can no longer understand anything. In answer to this pitiful outcry of your heart I say that this is not the time to reason things out, but to throw yourself at the feet of the Master and worship, pray, and simply stay there and wait. And when I say pray, I mean pray not with your lips but with your heart, offering the Lord the prayer of your tears and of your sorrow. "Pick up the crucifix and kiss it with

The Director of Souls

real faith, because Our Lord invites you to be crucified with Him. Let your will be subject to His and say over and over: "I desire what Thou desirest, O Lord." Once you are resigned to God's will, be calm and have no fear, for Our Lord certainly does not condemn tears or the cry of a suffering heart. He shed tears Himself and His Heart can appreciate the sorrow of your heart. Learn how to be patient and wait things out: He will make you see the inestimable price of this grief of yours that makes you like unto Him and is really a pledge of predestination and a sign of love."

Hidden with Christ

"*Believe, pray, and sacrifice yourself. Find God in the sanctifying commonplaces of everyday work.*"
CARDINAL MERRY DEL VAL

VIII

Hidden with Christ

XTERNALLY, Cardinal Merry del Val's life was simple and methodical, very much the same kind of daily life most of us lead by accepting calmly its obligations, its customs and conveniences, and taking an active part in ordinary, everyday events.

He was a man like anyone else who has a mind and a heart. Thus, there seemed to be in him nothing worthy of unusual admiration and nothing beyond the power of anyone to imitate. But if we look at his soul, we shall see vast horizons of virtue open up before our eyes, a panorama of sanctity one might never have suspected he possessed, proving once more that sanctity is not restricted to certain classes of people or to a special environment, but can blossom forth and flourish anywhere.

Under the guise of an ordinary life the Cardinal knew how to conceal no end of extraordinary virtues which he practiced continuously, reaching a high degree of interior perfection. Besides, he fulfilled regularly his daily duties with the humble joy and happiness that characterize the saints.

As someone has rightly pointed out, all his greatness really lies in this concealment, in the way he hid his virtue. Years ago, perhaps, one might have questioned which was greater, his active life in the Church or the interior life which flourished deep in the soul of this saintly man. Today, however, in the light of history and indisputable testimony, we can say that while he was a great man as a prince of the Church, he was certainly none the less great as a "man of God" in the full splendor of the most arduous Christian virtues.

Now we intend to lift, at least partially, the veil from

The Spiritual Life of Cardinal Merry del Val

those outstanding virtues that often went unnoticed even by the Cardinal's closest friends. In imitation of the saints he did his best to cultivate in both breadth and depth a harmonious blend of all virtues rather than stress any one virtue in particular.

Let us start with humility, the difficult conquest of oneself, the virtue of the truly great who see through the emptiness of this perishable and fleeting world.

Humility was the motto of the Borromeos, a family that gave the Church its full quota of saints and eminent prelates. Cardinal Merry del Val might well have chosen this same word for his own motto. From the very beginning his life was one of silence and sacrifice. His was a strong and simple faith, one that constantly made him feel humble in the eyes of God, and consequently in the eyes of his own conscience and in those of his fellow man.

In every event and circumstance of his life he tried to keep in mind those words of the Gospel, "Recline in the last place" (Luke 14, 10). Hence, he never entertained a high opinion of himself, and whenever he saw the bright path of honor and glory open up before him he always did his best to try to escape it. All he ever desired was to live forgotten and ignored by all, remembered and known by only one, that is to say, by God.

While still a student and not yet in Holy Orders, Leo XIII made him Secretary of the Extraordinary Papal Mission sent to London to offer the Pope's congratulations to Queen Victoria on the occasion of her golden jubilee. The young man, then studying at the Accademia dei Nobili Ecclesiastici, was quite upset over this singular honor bestowed upon him, and kneeling at the feet of the Pope, he humbly presented the following petition:

"Holy Father, my own desire in the matter would be not to leave the Academy and I am only too happy to yield this

Hidden with Christ

great honor to others who are more deserving than I."

The venerable Pontiff looked at him steadily for a moment or so, then gave him this solemn answer:

"And We have decided to send to London precisely one who does not desire to go there."

When appointed Papal Chamberlain, Merry del Val tried in every way possible to shun the honor that marked the first step in a career he had always feared. He explained all his reasons and exhausted every argument to let it be known that he did not like the idea of living at any court, even that of the Holy Father. He begged the Holy Father to change his decision, reiterating that his ideal had always been the salvation of souls in the humble ministry of the priesthood.

But the Pope had other big things in mind for him and his answer was simply this: "Obey!"

The youthful Monsignor was quite upset but he did not say a word. When he returned to the Academy, however, he sat down and wrote a letter to Father Dennis Sheil, a cousin of his, then living in Vienna. In it he reveals his true state of mind, saying: "Nothing could be more repugnant to me or more opposed to all my aspirations than this appointment. I would prefer it if the Lord gave me the grace of dying rather than inflict such a cross on me."

He accepted the difficult mission of Apostolic Delegate to Canada because the Holy Father had placed him under obedience. In a letter to Monsignor Joseph Broadhead he wrote: "I am to hurry off to Canada as Apostolic Delegate. . . . The Holy Father has placed me under obedience."

He did his best to get out of it when put in charge of the Accademia dei Nobili Ecclesiastici but could not, for the simple reason that the Holy Father would not heed his objections. Later on, at the death of Leo XIII, as soon as he heard that the Cardinal Dean, Oreglia di Santo Stefano, intended to propose his name to the Cardinals for

The Spiritual Life of Cardinal Merry del Val

nomination as Secretary of the Sacred College and consequently secretary of the coming conclave, he did all in his power to dissuade the venerable Cardinal on the grounds of inexperience and inability. But the Cardinal stood firm, for he was fully acquainted with the young Archbishop's virtue and piety and knew what he was capable of accomplishing. With deep humility Monsignor Merry del Val bowed both his mind and heart to what was for him the voice of God but, like a man who has lost his way, he immediately sat down and wrote to his dear friend in England, Monsignor Broadhead. It is a letter that clearly indicates his upset state of mind at the time:

> Vatican, Sala Borgia July 24, 1903
> I count on your prayers. I am installed in this most splendid abode, which is mine until after the conclave. I will not speak of myself except just to tell you that I am overwhelmed at the trust placed in me by the Sacred College. You will realize my feelings . . . the responsibility, and the work of having to be all of a sudden the acting Secretary of State . . . I can only leave all to God.

In like manner, every time a rumor would circulate around the Vatican that he was being mentioned as a worthy representative of the Holy See in this or that Nunciature, he would always reply with the remark: "A Nunciature would be like a tomb for me!"

On August 4, 1903, the Cardinal Patriarch of Venice ascended the Chair of Peter and took the name of Pius X. Monsignor Merry del Val, who had managed to perfection the running of the conclave, was anxiously awaiting the moment when he could step aside from the heavy burden of this new office.

Hidden with Christ

From hour to hour he held himself in readiness to step down from his position in favor of the Secretary of State whom the new Pope would appoint as soon as he would make up his mind in the matter.

This remarkable frame of mind is reflected in a letter he wrote at that time to Monsignor Broadhead:

MY DEAR OLD FRIEND:
This is a most unenviable position. How any man alive, whether he be dressed in red or purple, can wish to occupy it is more than I can understand. I go on from day to day. . . . I need hardly say that not a few are anxious to see me replaced. If they only knew how I am longing for that, but to many I must appear as clinging to the post.

A short while later, almost on the eve of his appointment as Secretary of State, he again expressed this same humble feeling in the matter when writing to the Mother Superior of the Little Company of Mary: "I hope to be granted the favor of leaving this office which is so little in keeping with my desires."

While St. Pius X was still pondering about choosing a Secretary of State, some of the Cardinals, it seems, had already settled on Merry del Val and did their best to push his nomination with the new Pope. The young Pro-Secretary of State soon became aware of what was going on and without further delay went to a prelate who enjoyed the Pope's confidence and said: "In my name tell the Holy Father that I know all about what is being done to have him appoint me Secretary of State. Point out to him, however, that I am too young and not suited for such a position and, consequently, he should consider someone else."

It was so completely foreign to his nature to think about himself that he even went to the Holy Father a day or so later and suggested that a certain eminent Cardinal of the

The Spiritual Life of Cardinal Merry del Val

Curia would make an excellent Secretary of State.

St. Pius X heard and observed all that went on about him while waiting for an inspiration from God in the matter. He had become fully acquainted with the virtues and superior qualities of his Pro-Secretary of State; so, one morning when giving him his usual bundle of official documents, he said:

"Monsignor, there is also something here for you!"

Archbishop Merry del Val went down to his own apartment and got right to work. In the course of handling the documents his eye fell upon an envelope addressed to him in the handwriting of the Holy Father. He had no reason to think it other than official business, so he opened it rather indifferently, unfolded the sheet of paper, and there he read about his appointment as both Secretary of State and Cardinal. Surprised and amazed at what he read, he hesitated a moment in silent prayer then went right up to see the Holy Father again. A brief but touching meeting took place between St. Pius X and his Prime Minister. Archbishop Merry del Val told the Pope how upset he was over the news, how the thought of holding such an office filled him with trepidation. He made use of every argument to try and have the appointment revoked. His deep humility really came to the fore as he begged the Pope to be relieved of a burden and of a responsibility that truly frightened him.

St. Pius X stood by his decision, however, and exhorted him to accept the cross as the Lord gave it to him; he assured him that his appointment was in full conformity with the will of God.

The fact that Merry del Val had been suddenly promoted to the high office of Secretary of State and at the same time created a Cardinal when just thirty-eight years of age was something that his ingrained humility took right in stride. When preparations were being made for his elevation to the Cardinalate, one of his assistants testified that it was not

Hidden with Christ

easy to persuade him to have his measurements taken for his Cardinal's robes. The change of color from purple to red seemed almost to surprise him and he did not fully realize that he had been created a Cardinal until the Consistory when he had to actually put on the red robes.

In his address at the Consistory, when thanking the Pope for having bestowed the Cardinalate upon him, he extolled the merits of Bishop Callegari of Mantua, who had received the Red Hat at the same Consistory, and concluded by saying: "I have little or nothing to offer Your Holiness on this happy occasion as the fruit of my labors or that might justify the supreme honor being bestowed upon me today."

So too, when a certain person, in congratulating him on his appointment as Secretary of State, remarked: "What a heavy cross the Lord has placed upon your shoulders!" he answered: "You are the only person who has said the real truth of the matter." When the Bishop of Poitiers offered congratulations on the same appointment, Merry del Val quoted the words of St. John the Baptist, applying them to himself and the Holy Father, saying: "He must increase, but I must decrease" (John 3, 30).

Completely detached as he was from the things of the world, the Cardinal never became vain. Honors meant absolutely nothing to him and he never aspired to any position of authority, for he looked at everything from the viewpoint of eternity and always kept in mind an admonition he himself had written:

"There is always danger for our eternal salvation when we give orders; it is not that way, on the contrary, when we obey. It is very difficult for us to withstand the assaults of pride when we impose our will on others. Let us, therefore, learn to fear rather than desire honors or superiority, for they are nothing but a long and painful martyrdom. A true priest puts up with them but he most certainly does not seek

The Spiritual Life of Cardinal Merry del Val

them.

When Cardinal Rampolla died on December 12, 1913, the question arose as to who would take his place as Archpriest of the Vatican Basilica. In and around the Vatican Cardinal Merry del Val's name was mentioned as the unanimous choice. But the rumor had scarcely started to circulate before the Pope made up his mind to bestow that great honor upon his Secretary of State. As soon as the humble Cardinal heard his name being mentioned, his first thought was of his own unworthiness. He went to Monsignor Ungherini who enjoyed the Pope's confidence and begged him to ask the Holy Father to consider some other Cardinal who would be, as he put it in his humility, "better suited and more worthy."

He finally agreed to accept only when he learned that he would have hurt the Pope's feelings if he refused the appointment. St. Pius X, it seems, wanted this to serve as a final token and testimonial of the affection and gratitude he bore his Secretary of State.

The Cardinal was a man of the Church and a priest of God in the fullest and highest sense of the word. There was only one honor he ever desired; all through his life he aspired to greatness in but one thing, the priestly ministry for the salvation of souls.

The following letter, written while he was President of the Pontifical Academy of Nobles, shows that the passion of his whole life was "Give me souls; take away all else!"

MOST HOLY FATHER,

Prostrate at the feet of Your Holiness, with sentiments of filial submission I come to make known to You a truly heartfelt desire of mine and earnestly beg a favor which, in my eyes, represents the most the paternal goodness of Your Holiness could ever do for the humblest of His

Hidden with Christ

children.

Until now I have never asked Your Holiness for anything for myself: this is the first favor I now ask, and perhaps it will be the last.

I would like Your Holiness to grant me permission to resign from the office I now hold, however unworthily, in the Accademia Ecclesiastici and let me retire to Trastevere or to some other section of Rome, where, free from all other responsibilities, I could dedicate myself completely to the priestly ministry in the midst of the people, and at the same time devote myself to the spiritual welfare of foreigners in Rome, especially those who speak the English language.

I do not have great sources of income but what I get from my family is adequate for me to live on and I neither ask for nor want anything more.

This decision will perhaps cause some to wonder and will probably be interpreted differently by those that do not know me; but I shall be happy to accept the consequences, convinced as I am that I am doing something pleasing to the Lord.

There is absolutely nothing at the Accademia that I find displeasing, and, as a matter of fact, rather than see myself promoted to other assignments I would be happy to stay in this institution to the end of my life. But if Your Holiness would see fit to grant me the favor I have asked my happiness would be complete and I would be forever grateful to Your Holiness.

My Holy Father, I place this prayerful request of mine at Your feet, and, with sentiments of perfect submission to Your will, I remain,

The most humble and obedient child of Your Holiness,
          RAPHAEL MERRY DEL VAL

Titular Archbishop of Nicaea

December 18, 1901

The Spiritual Life of Cardinal Merry del Val

He was a great man, but he himself remained unaware of his greatness. He loved silence, "simplicity and a life hidden in his work for the salvation of souls." A mantle of secrecy shrouded even the more solemn events of his life and his closest friends and associates were unaware of them. He shunned all noisy celebrations and shied away from any public or private demonstration that might be looked on as a tribute to his outstanding merits, for all such honorary manifestations seemed to him nothing more than bright little clouds that are dispersed by the first gust of wind that comes along.

For the silver jubilee of his ordination he stayed with his boys in Trastevere. A few days later, on January 4, 1913, he wrote to a prominent gentleman in Rome a letter that gives us some idea of the depth of his humility: "When I reflect upon the sublime dignity of the priesthood and when I reflect upon the responsibility that goes with it, upon the duties it imposes, and when I see what I should have done during these twenty-five years and have not done, I seem to lose all desire to celebrate and to receive congratulations, but all I want to do is go off in some corner of the earth to weep over my shortcomings and prepare myself for eternity."

The Vatican Chapter put so much pressure upon him in 1925 that he finally yielded to their requests and celebrated Solemn Mass in St. Peter's in commemoration of his silver jubilee as a bishop. A great number of Cardinals honored him by their presence at the Mass. A pious woman whom the Cardinal had brought into the Church later wrote to him and mentioned the deep impression made on her by this solemn and impressive ceremony. The Cardinal's comment in return was: "That ceremony made me think of my funeral at which, in all probability, those Cardinals will be present."

Hidden with Christ

In 1928, however, when his friends and admirers expressed their desire of having a solemn celebration in honor of his jubilee as a Cardinal, he would not allow it. All he had was a private blessing of the Holy Father and the singing of a simple Te Deum.

He was never one to go in search of praise. Whenever anyone would praise him he used to dismiss it with a shake of his head and say: "This is something that I do not like." He never talked about himself or put his culture and erudition on display. He kept constantly under wraps his truly grand qualities of both mind and heart.

Being opposed as he was to any form of display, the Cardinal naturally had little or no time for portraits.

He occasionally posed for a photographer but purely out of courtesy and condescension. He never wanted to spend so much as a penny for his own pictures, saying that such a thing would cause him scruples and that he could never understand how anyone could keep a picture of himself right in his own drawing room.

There was never the slightest bit of ostentation about him. The papal basilicas, the Holy Stairs at the Lateran, the station churches during Lent, the tombs of the martyrs, were places where he was very often seen praying in the midst of the faithful dressed as a simple priest.

During the service one year at the Church of Sts. John and Paul he was seen on his knees praying in a corner of the church. One of the Passionist Fathers who staffed the church recognized him and hurried over to bring him a cushion, but the Cardinal very politely refused it.

On another occasion, in the Vatican Basilica he was seen one afternoon kneeling on the bare pavement in profound recollection before the Blessed Sacrament solemnly exposed for the Forty Hours' Adoration.

The Spiritual Life of Cardinal Merry del Val

He never liked having people stand on ceremony with him, so whenever he traveled outside of Rome he usually wore his black cassock so that there was absolutely nothing about him to betray his high rank in the Church.

His habit of traveling incognito often gave rise to amusing and even touching incidents. Thus, one morning during the summer of 1924 it so happened he was in the Church of the Servants of Mary at Pesaro. He entered the sacristy and saw several priests awaiting their turn to say Mass. Shortly, there was an opening at one of the altars and a priest standing nearby came up to him and whispered: "Father, so as not to lose time, we usually serve Mass for one another, and with your permission I would like to say Mass first since I must get back to my parish." The Cardinal was happy to go along with the arrangement and, as a result, he served Mass for the parish priest.

He was even more truly humble deep down in his soul than he was aristocratic by name and blood. He liked nothing more than to take off all the insignia of his high office and spend his time with the plain people, with the poor, with the uneducated country folk. He liked the simplicity of their language and loved to talk and listen to them. He would encourage and comfort them, and even help them sometimes in their hard, manual labor. That is the way he is remembered by the people in Trastevere, by the shepherds in the Dolomites, by the simple mountain folk from around Arabba, by the villagers of Riese—where St. Pius X was born and raised—and by the fishermen at the lake of Piediluco in the valley of Rieti.

But, after all, this should come as no great surprise, for this same man, writing to his pious mother early in his career, once referred to himself as "something small and insignificant"; and when presenting his opinions as

Hidden with Christ

Consultor of the Sacred Congregation of the Index, if anyone praised his work for its solid exposition of doctrine and its elegant style, he would minimize his efforts, saying: "I am not worth much and there is little that I know how to do." When Titular Archbishop of Nicaea and President of the Accademia dei Nobili Ecclesiastici he did not hesitate to call himself once a "useless piece of furniture."

He was the Prime Minister of the most powerful Sovereign on earth, but talking to the countless thousands of pilgrims that converged upon Rome he used to refer to himself as the "humble Secretary of State of the Holy Father."

As Secretary of State and intimate collaborator in the many achievements of a pontificate dedicated to "restoring all things in Christ" he hid himself in order that the work and person of his Pope might stand out in bolder relief. He was happy with his role of self-effacement and content to tell God all about it in the course of his mystical colloquies, saying: "O Lord, I am nothing, but this nothing worships Thee."

As Archpriest of the Vatican Basilica he was a truly tireless worker, one who gave his all in promoting the splendor and decorum of the greatest church of Christianity, but in his address to the Vatican Chapter on the occasion of his episcopal jubilee he confessed with deep humility: "I feel that I have done but very little."

He was above all the pious priest who became little in his own eyes and could thus exclaim from the mystical heights of prayer: "Change my heart, O Jesus, abased for love of me! Disclose to my spirit the supreme value of Thy holy humiliations. May I begin today, enlightened by Thy light, to destroy that portion of the old Adam which yet lives whole and entire within me, for the great cause of my wretchedness is the constant hindrance that I put in the way

The Spiritual Life of Cardinal Merry del Val

of Thy love."

Every morning after Mass he would steep his soul in a meditation on our "human nothingness" and beg God to set him free from the desire of being honored and from the fear of being humiliated. We are referring here to his daily recitation of his "Litany of Humility":

> O Jesus, meek and humble of heart, hear me.
> From the desire of being esteemed,
> deliver me, O Jesus.
> From the desire of being loved,
> deliver me, O Jesus.
> From the desire of being extolled,
> deliver me, O Jesus.
> From the desire of being honored,
> deliver me, O Jesus.
> From the desire of being praised,
> deliver me, O Jesus.
> From the desire of being preferred to others,
> deliver me, O Jesus.
> From the desire of being consulted,
> deliver me, O Jesus.
> From the desire of being approved,
> deliver me, O Jesus.
> From the fear of being humiliated,
> deliver me, O Jesus.
> From the fear of being despised,
> deliver me, O Jesus.
> From the fear of suffering rebukes,
> deliver me, O Jesus.
> From the fear of being calumniated,
> deliver me, O Jesus.
> From the fear of being forgotten,
> deliver me, O Jesus

Hidden with Christ

From the fear of being ridiculed,
deliver me, O Jesus
From the fear of being wronged,
deliver me, O Jesus
From the fear of being suspected,
deliver me, O Jesus.

That others may be loved more than I,
Jesus, grant me the grace to desire it.
That others may be esteemed more than I
Jesus, grant me the grace to desire it.
That in the opinion of the world, others may increase and I may decrease
Jesus, grant me the grace to desire it.
That others may be chosen and I set aside,
Jesus, grant me the grace to desire it.
That others may be praised and I unnoticed,
Jesus, grant me the grace to desire it.
That others may be preferred to me in everything,
Jesus, grant me the grace to desire it.
That others may become holier than I, provided that I may become as holy as I should,
Jesus, grant me the grace to desire it.

This was the daily prayer of that saintly Cardinal who, almost on the threshold of eternity, asked the favor of being put to rest next to the Pope whom he had loved and served with every fiber of his being. In his will he also requested that his tomb be completely unadorned except for his name and these words drawn from Sacred Scripture: "Give me souls; take away all else!"

In the Footsteps of the Saints

"Cut away here, O my Jesus; burn and destroy here all there is in me that is not Thine."
CARDINAL MERRY DEL VAL

IX

In the Footsteps of the Saints

IKE all great souls, Cardinal Merry del Val had a passion for charity that knew no limits; merciful charity that helps a person without humiliating him; pious charity inspired not by any human motives but only out of love for God.

"Lavishly he gives to the poor" (Ps. 111, 9). Cardinal Merry del Val loved the poor and needy, all those weighed down with any sort of misfortune. He loved them silently and in humility, with utmost secrecy because he loved humble charity, the kind that disarms any form of pride and wins out over egotism.

Those he helped were never supposed to know his name; the benefactor had to remain known only to God. Whether others saw or did not see meant absolutely nothing to him; all that mattered was knowing that there was a divine eye that saw what he did. He knew that charity is a treasure not to be bought or sold but given away, and that was enough. Hence, one of his truly outstanding characteristics was his ability to conceal the charity that flowed so generously from his hands.

During the time he was Titular Archbishop of Nicaea, he was constantly called upon to administer Confirmation, especially in the more thickly populated quarters of Rome. And it was always a pleasure for him, for he considered it an honor and joy to be thrown into contact with those that are shunned or looked down upon by an egotistical world. He would often go to homes that were nothing more than hovels to confirm sick children. He would encourage and bless them; then, when the ceremony was over and while their relatives all flocked around to kiss his hand, with a tender smile and without letting anyone notice it he would

The Spiritual Life of Cardinal Merry del Val

slip a generous contribution into the hand of one of the parents.

When going out for a walk he always carried some money with him; then, when he met some poor person he would slip the money into his hand with such dexterity that not even a person walking along with him could notice it.

It happened more than once that young people in need who lacked the nerve to ask him for anything suddenly found themselves with money in their pocket; it had been put there by the Cardinal without their even knowing it.

One day he went to the bedside of a young man who was seriously ill. The Cardinal had heard about the poverty of the man's family, and with his usual delicacy and dexterity he slipped under the sick man's pillow an envelope containing a considerable amount of money. At the time no one noticed his kind gesture. But the next morning when the young man discovered the envelope with the money he immediately thought of the Cardinal and right away sent a member of the family over to thank him. "But why thank me," said the Cardinal, "when you don't know who it was that gave you the envelope? Thank the Lord who has watched over you."

Even when he was a young Monsignor his chief concern was to help the poor but at the same time to remain unknown. So he used to make his way through the crooked streets and hidden alleyways of Rome in search of those nameless, forgotten derelicts who were afraid to show themselves in public for fear of being refused an alms.

One winter evening he was seen walking along in a terrible rainstorm in the ordinary dress of a priest. He went down an obscure little street, climbed a dark, rickety stairway, and knocked on a door. With an envelope in his hand he said: "This is the answer to the letter you wrote today." He had just gotten a letter asking for help and that

In the Footsteps of the Saints

was his way of replying. It is a touching episode, Christian in the highest sense of the word, and there were many others like it.

There were many poor people who were spared the embarrassment of having to accept an alms and there were others who never even knew who was helping them. They discovered who their unknown benefactor was only when his death put an end to the flow of his charity.

One day he was asked to help a woman who had been suddenly reduced to a state of utter poverty. He came to her assistance immediately, not once but many times, but it was always done through a third person and surrounded with utmost secrecy. The woman never knew the name of her illustrious benefactor until after the Cardinal's death.

A high-ranking Roman prelate who knew Merry del Val intimately from the time he was a student at the Pontifical Academy testified as follows: "There were no limits to our Cardinal's charity nor were there ever any conditions attached to it. I have come to this conclusion only after making an accurate investigation among all those who had anything to do with him." This comes as no great surprise when one bears in mind that the Cardinal once took the sheets and mattress from his own bed and gave them to a poor family. The Cardinal's charity knew no limits for he looked on it as an apostolate for the salvation of souls.

"When a poor person," he once wrote, "sees a priest approach him with consideration for his misery and sympathy for his suffering it will be easy for him to recognize the truth that lies hidden beneath the priest's habit of love."

On July 28, 1934, the Provincial Superior of the Institute of the Blessed Virgin Mary in Bressanone wrote as follows:

"The last time I saw the Cardinal was on June 18, 1929, and I asked him to put in a good word with certain

The Spiritual Life of Cardinal Merry del Val

authorities for a pressing work of charity. He expressed his regret at not being able to do so immediately; then he took out his purse and completely emptied it before my eyes, apologizing because there was not more in it. All he had was six hundred lire!"

A Canon of the Vatican Basilica made this statement:

"No one ever had recourse to him in vain; no one ever left him without getting some sort of help and comfort. He gave to all, and in order to give even more he imposed upon himself a way of life that was parsimonious and at times even downright austere. He was always so courteous and genteel in exercising his charity that it seemed as if he were the one accepting it."

Bishops hard at work in the apostolic fields of China turned to him for help and always got it. He was the benefactor of countless priests struggling with the hardships of life; they could always count on him for help. Because of him hundreds of jobless workers were assured of always having something to eat, and the clergy, the choir members, the Sampietrini of the Vatican Basilica could turn to him in their domestic troubles and find help, sometimes even without having to ask for it. He helped others by secretly selling one of his episcopal rings at London in 1917, at a time when the First World War was devastating Europe.

Some of those he had helped proved ungrateful and forgot all about the favors they had received. They did not know, however, that he forgave them and continued helping them, as if their ingratitude were an added incentive to his generosity.

One day an urgent request was lodged with the Cardinal to help a poor sick priest. He immediately came to the priest's assistance with a generous offering but did not even receive an acknowledgment. There was no expression whatsoever of gratitude. The Cardinal showed his

In the Footsteps of the Saints

disappointment merely by saying: "Even Our Lord very often is not thanked for the favors He bestows upon men."

The parish priests of many churches in Rome could all bear witness to the charity of the Cardinal. Monsignor de Angelis, the parish priest of St. Peter's, wrote a letter on October 21, 1930, in which he testifies: "It seems to me that among the many extraordinary virtues that adorned the soul of our beloved Cardinal, the one that stood out more than all others was his charity and compassion for the poor.

"I can attest to this because I often acted as intermediary in the distribution of his charity; he was always ready to give prompt and generous assistance. When it was a question of families of means that had become destitute he used to give hundreds of lire: and so also to poor widows, to orphans, and to poor students.

"I know for a fact that besides the many contributions he made to the poor in my parish he was also generous in helping the poor of other parishes both in and outside of Rome.

"This much is known to me: the good Lord alone knows how much else he did."

It was with considerable feeling that Monsignor Bernabai, a Canon at St. Peter's, stated:

"I think back and remember all the outstanding charitable deeds our beloved and unforgettable Cardinal Archpriest constantly performed for the poor and needy. 'Yes, Monsignor,' he used to say to me when I would draw his attention to some pitiful case, and immediately generous provision would be made for the person mentioned.

"'I shall be your almsgiver!' I said to him with a smile one day when he had given me a sum of money to be delivered to three sisters in need of help."

The good people of Trastevere still remember the inexhaustible charity of the pious Cardinal. For forty years

The Spiritual Life of Cardinal Merry del Val

he walked through the streets of this section of Rome generously distributing charity in all its forms, helping families, comforting the downtrodden, and bringing consolation to the victims of misfortune. Bearing witness to this fact are all those young men he educated in his "Pious Association of the Sacred Heart of Jesus." One of these, Virgilio Signori, recalling precious memories of his earlier years writes as follows:

"It requires no great effort of the imagination for us who knew and loved him to go back in spirit to those bygone days and still see Cardinal Merry del Val walking along through the old streets of Trastevere where there was so much poverty. We can still see him entering the homes of those in need and bringing them the smile of his charity. He continued to help the poor just as he had done in the early years of his life, even when he was Vice President of the "Conferences of St. Vincent de Paul" at St. Michael's College in Brussels, where he was enrolled as a student in 1878.

"He gave without ever humiliating anyone because there was so much refinement and modesty attached to the way in which he distributed his charity. His exquisite delicacy could well be expressed in a phrase that seems to have been coined just for him: 'He could descend without ever lowering himself.'

"But how can anyone try to add up all his alms deeds when they were continuous and almost without number?

"It was he who paid the rent for families unable to pay it. It was he who found work for those that did not know how or where to find it. He was the one who went out and procured employment for needy young men. Finally, it was he who, disregarding the sacrifice entailed or the expenses involved, would provide the sick, the infirm, and the invalids with care, support, and medicines."

In the Footsteps of the Saints

Mr. Signori then goes on to say: "But the moral and spiritual assistance which the Cardinal showed those of Trastevere, not to mention the material aid he lavished upon them, really reached its peak during the tragic period of the First World War. Many of his boys were called to the front in defense of their country. All those young men who had been taught by the Cardinal to love goodness and virtue left fully aware of their duty; not much was said as they left but you could see how proud they were of their eminent father's parting words of comfort and blessing.

"During these anxious times the Cardinal offered Holy Mass every morning for those of his boys who were at the front. And they maintain that they felt the blessing of their spiritual father uplifting and strengthening them with the certainty that God was with them.

"During the disastrous retreat in October of 1917, when no news came for weeks, the Cardinal was an angel of comfort to many fathers and mothers who were enduring the agonies of a heartbreaking suspense. He anxiously searched the lists of dead, wounded, or missing which came to the Vatican, and when he saw the name of one of his boys he set off at once to break the news to the family and to comfort them as he alone knew how.

"Because of this charity, which had become proverbial, they all used to call him their 'Angel of Mercy,' their 'Saint Raphael.' The title 'His Eminence' could apply to only one person so far as the people of Trastevere were concerned—Cardinal Merry del Val."

At his death people mourned him everywhere. "Cardinal Merry del Val is dead. . . . Poor Trastevere!" was the remark made by a gentleman in Rome on reading the news of the Cardinal's death. "You have lost your father," Cardinal Bisleti told the young men of the "Pious Association of the Sacred Heart of Jesus in Trastevere."

The Spiritual Life of Cardinal Merry del Val

"What a misfortune! Think of all the families in Trastevere that will be affected by this death. It is like having a death in your own family. It is hard to think about it without weeping!" was the comment made by many mothers and fathers. On the lips of all you could almost hear the glorious words of Dante Alighieri:

> And if the world did know the heart he had,
> 'Twould deem the praise it yields him scantly dealt.
> (PARADISE VI, 140-141.)

The Cardinal always wanted charity to be an essential part of the more solemn moments of his life. On the day of his episcopal consecration his concern was not with applause or honors but with works of mercy and of Christian charity. Breaking the age-old custom of receptions and "refreshments," he gave a dinner for two hundred poor people and clothing for all of them. With a generous contribution he also brought comfort and consolation to an old woman who had been sick for some time.

On his elevation to the Cardinalate he clothed and fed many who were completely destitute. And when he celebrated his silver jubilee as a bishop he did just what he had done twenty-five years before, he helped and comforted those in need.

On December 28, 1908, when a terrible earthquake razed to the ground the two flourishing cities, Reggio Calabria and Messina, his was the first name to appear in a list of offerings collected by a special Committee of the Catholic Young Men of Italy. He also quickly transformed the Hospice of Santa Maria in Vaticano into a welcome place of refuge for the thousands of orphans and unfortunates that came pouring into the City of Rome. St. Pius X welcomed them all and Cardinal Merry del Val personally supervised

In the Footsteps of the Saints

the management of the hospice.

In 1917 the relatives and family friends of St. Pius X were forced to flee their home in the face of an enemy attack and came to Rome in search of comfort and relief. If they had a roof over their heads and some food to eat at that time it was precisely because of the Cardinal.

Wherever there was a good cause to espouse in either the religious or the social field the Cardinal was always on hand like the "good soldier of Christ" (2 Tim. 2, 3).

The Kitchens for the Poor at St. Peter's, the Conferences of St. Vincent de Paul, and the Little House of Peace for abandoned children of Rome still recall the generosity and goodness of his heart. He will never be forgotten by those stricken and driven from their homes by the disastrous flood of 1926 that devastated the rich fields in the valley of Rieti. People still remember the generous donations he made to the works of the Propagation of the Faith, of Ecclesiastical Vocations, of Perpetual Adoration, of Christian Doctrine in the Parishes of Rome, and of the Archconfraternity of the Madonna del Carmine in Trastevere. The keen interest he showed and the generous material assistance he gave the Society for Converts from Anglicanism will never be forgotten. This society originated in London for the purpose of trying to solve some of the problems of life confronting those former Anglican ministers who, although they had become priests, were nevertheless often faced with poverty and extremely difficult living conditions.

Here is the testimony of one of the prominent members of this Society, F. W. Chambers. He paid a visit to the Cardinal in October, 1925, and on March 7, 1930, wrote as follows in the London *Catholic Times:*

> One Sunday morning I arrived at the Palazzo of Santa Marta and was immediately ushered into the

The Spiritual Life of Cardinal Merry del Val

Cardinal's presence. We talked about the Society, about conversions in general, and about Anglicanism. Nobody was better informed than he on these topics. After forty minutes I got up to leave. His Eminence accompanied me to the door where there were a lot of people waiting to see him. But before I went out, speaking with reference to conversions among the Anglican clergy, he made a remark that I shall never forget: "Mr. Chambers, I take my hat off to these heroic men. I am not worthy to polish their shoes: they are indeed our modern martyrs!" That is what the Cardinal told me with that deep humility which characterizes all true greatness. Then, shortly after my return to England, he sent me a check for thirty pounds and from that time on became a regular contributor to the Society.

With the death of Cardinal Merry del Val our Society lost one of its most generous supporters. May he rest in peace, and may he continue to pray for "this truly exquisite work of charity" as the Holy Father has defined it.

The pious Cardinal's entire life was completely interwoven with charity and so too was his death.

His will, written when almost on the very threshold of eternity, is his final answer to that insatiable cry welling up from the depths of his soul: "Give me souls; take away all else!" He left everything he had to the Sacred Congregation of Propaganda in behalf of poor missions. His bequests included nothing that he had received from the Church in the way of salary because that passed right through his hands. He left what he had inherited from his family and was, therefore, his to dispose of as he saw fit. Thus, even after his death he continued to carry on his apostolate for the salvation of souls and certainly merited for himself the

In the Footsteps of the Saints

title of "Propagator of the Faith."

In the month of February, the last he was to spend on earth, he put in an order for a special orthopedic apparatus and had it sent to a poor invalid, the father of a large family. On Sunday, February 23rd, he sent off a liberal donation to the St. Vincent de Paul Conference of the parish of St. Peter's and prepared an envelope with some Mass intentions for a priest whom he took care of regularly.

Three days later, after the Cardinal had died, the envelope was given to the priest. He was so touched by it that he burst out crying and said: "After having helped me so much during life, the saintly Cardinal helps me even after his death. May God bless him!"

The Cardinal had been endowed by nature with a forceful disposition and an ardent temperament but through unceasing struggle he succeeded in acquiring a serene and imperturbable mind. One of his old classmates in St. Michael's College at Brussels wrote: "Although he had an ardent temperament, I never noticed in him either an outburst of temper, or a complaint, or any sort of argument with his classmates—an obvious indication of the wonderful control he had over himself at all times."

Another classmate, of the Accademia dei Nobili Ecclesiastici, stated: "Young Merry del Val had an ardent temperament and a sensitive heart that could easily have yielded to the impulses of his nature. But he controlled and conquered himself in silence. He was never heard to complain or talk about anything that bothered him and he never returned evil for evil. He would suffer in silence, content and happy to be able to offer up something to God. Gradually he acquired that uniformity of character and that serene amiableness that distinguished him all through life."

One who knew him from his earliest years in Rome

The Spiritual Life of Cardinal Merry del Val

made the following statement:

"He fulfilled the obligations of his duties with complete mastery both of himself and of his time; he possessed that rare aptitude of being able to move about with equal ease and naturalness in the midst of the most diversified occupations. He never let them tire his patience no matter how prolonged they might be, nor did he allow any interruption to upset his calm."

Because he was meek and humble our Cardinal knew how to forgive and forget. A Spanish anarchist who was notorious for the boisterous insults he hurled at the Pope and at his Secretary of State was moved by the grace of God and came to Rome to seek forgiveness. He presented himself to the Cardinal and, kneeling down, gave every indication of true repentance and made a full confession of his evil deeds. The Cardinal was taken by surprise and looked at him for a moment: then he helped the man to rise and assured him that he had already forgiven and forgotten everything.

There was trouble everywhere, it seemed, at the time St. Pius X began his pontificate. Those were times of strife and treachery, and, as at all such decisive moments of history, an absolute stand had to be taken; a course had to be followed without any weakness or hesitation; quick and sure measures had to be taken to safeguard the Faith, the freedom of the Church and the integrity of Catholic thought.

On all sides the Church was faced with bitter sectarian hatred. French Masonry, using various diplomatic pretexts, was endeavoring to create a government hostile to the Church. Spain and Portugal were considering the enactment of laws that would deprive bishops and priests of their rights and freedom. Mexico and Ecuador, departing from their age-old traditions, were both faced with the same dilemma:

In the Footsteps of the Saints

either the absolute domination of the state or a violent renewal of bitter conflict with the Apostolic See. Russia showed ever-increasing hostility by putting obstacles in the way of appointing bishops to Russian Sees. Austria and Germany tried to hinder the Church's progress in the religious as well as the social field. In Italy an ugly anticlerical movement had broken out, using as its chief weapon slander and calumny against the Church and religious communities.

Such were the troublesome times in the midst of which Cardinal Merry del Val found himself. They were to cause him many tribulations and heartaches, but at the same time they served to emphasize the man's great courage, solid virtue, and fearless heart.

St. Pius X had foretold that the shadow of the cross would mark the course of his pontificate by saying to the Cardinal: "We shall work together and suffer together out of love for the Church." The Cardinal was to suffer from scorching criticism by the enemies of the Church and to be the target of vilification and abuse, so that St. Pius X was often to say: "Poor Merry del Val!"

As the writer Prati stated: "What happened to Cardinal Merry del Val has always happened to the Secretary of State of the Holy See. The adversaries of Pius X, whose popularity increased from year to year, made his Secretary of State bear the brunt of all their criticisms and recriminations against the Pontiff.

"Cardinal Merry del Val came in for a special share of abuse, for at the time of Pius X many people entertained the false idea that the saintly Pontiff was just a `kind old country parish priest' who detested politics and did nothing but pray, leaving the government of the Church to his Secretary of State.

The Spiritual Life of Cardinal Merry del Val

"But Pius X, notwithstanding his evangelical kindness and virtue, was an energetic and inflexible Pope, and all the severe but providential measures that were taken during his pontificate were firmly willed by him and energetically carried out by him with the intelligent and loyal collaboration of his Secretary of State."

History will one day tell the full story. At the present time we can say that not a single event, no pressure ever put on him by any political party or secular power ever intimidated or swayed the Cardinal Secretary of State of St. Pius X. When the going was roughest and his trials reached their peak, he never knew the meaning of compromise or capitulation.

Prepared for every test and every crisis, he assumed his share of responsibility before both God and men that the Church might shine everywhere with the bright light of integrity.

The Cardinal Secretary of State of St. Pius X was not born poor, but he learned how to become poor because he was humble. He seemed aware of that fact himself for, during a talk to a group of novices, he made the remark: "The spirit of poverty is the highest expression of humility.

The craving for money and the attachment to riches never touched his heart, and the fever of earthly goods, as St. Augustine would say, never tormented him. Amidst all the splendor of two papal courts he always looked and acted the part of the man of God, "the rich man found without fault, who turns not aside after gain!" (Ecclus. 31, 8).

Cardinal Canali, who was Merry del Val's daily companion for almost thirty years, mentions the following incident. When St. Pius X decided to make him a Cardinal, he sent him twenty-five thousand lire with a personal note stating that the money was to defray any expenses he might

In the Footsteps of the Saints

have to meet in keeping with his promotion to this high office. The Cardinal was deeply touched by the gesture but tactfully let it be known to the Pope that he did not need the money because his parents would take care of all the expenses incidental to his promotion. St. Pius X, however, insisted once more that he take the money, particularly in view of the fact that he had not kept a cent for himself since the day he was appointed secretary of the conclave. To show his gratitude and regard for the Pope, the Cardinal finally consented to accept the money, but he soon got rid of it. A Spanish priest of considerable means had decided that he wanted to renovate the second floor of the Apostolic Palace and the Cardinal turned over his money for the installation of a heating unit in the Pope's own apartment.

Cardinal Merry del Val had helped to establish the Spanish College in Rome, and in 1925, on the occasion of his silver jubilee as a bishop, it wanted to honor him by a gift of twenty-five thousand lire. The Cardinal greatly appreciated the thoughtfulness behind the gift but immediately took the money and with it set up two burses in the same college for the maintenance of poor students.

In 1929, when the Holy See increased the monthly allowance for Cardinals working in the Roman Curia, a special increase was given those Cardinals in charge of Sacred Congregations or Ecclesiastical Tribunals. Cardinal Merry del Val turned over to the Church the increase that was due him as Secretary of the Supreme Sacred Congregation of the Holy Office; he then took what was coming to him as a Cardinal of the Curia and used it to raise the salaries of his household staff.

Since he was detached from earthly possessions, he never accumulated any wealth or, for that matter, never even set aside a penny for himself. Under St. Pius X, for eleven years he acted as President of the Commission for the

The Spiritual Life of Cardinal Merry del Val

Administration of the Goods of the Holy See, as Prefect of the Sacred Apostolic Palace, and as Secretary of State. But when at the death of his beloved Pontiff he had to renovate the ancient Palazzina of Santa Marta where he was supposed to live as the new Archpriest of the Vatican Basilica, he had to turn to his father for financial assistance.

In 1922, when he had to get new Cardinalitial robes, he had to turn to his mother for help because his entire salary always finished up in the hands of the poor.

When it came to the administration of Church money, especially the handling of Peter's Pence, the Cardinal was strict almost to the point of scrupulosity. Cardinal Canali, who, as mentioned above, was with Merry del Val for almost thirty years, goes on record as follows:

"Never once did it happen during the whole time that he was Secretary of State that he ever took so much as a single lira of money belonging to the Holy See, even if it was a question of giving an alms or making a charitable contribution of any sort. He always gave as much of his own money as he could. It was pointed out to him that since these were not personal concerns, but official ones, he could use his own discretion, as indeed the Holy Father himself had authorized him to do. But it was useless to try to convince him."

In 1908 St. Pius X made an earnest appeal to Catholics all over the world to come to the aid of the victims of an earthquake that had completely wiped out many cities and towns in Calabria and Sicily. All the money that reached the Vatican in ever-increasing amounts during those sad days passed through the hands of the Cardinal Secretary of State. He prepared the lists of the offerings which he then presented to the Pope. But when the offerings did not come out in a round figure, quite often he made up the difference out of his own money.

In the Footsteps of the Saints

At the time people from all over the world were making contributions for the monument to Pius X in the Vatican Basilica, he wrote personally to thank all who had contributed. But he paid the postage out of his own pocket, and in some cases it was considerable. He did not want to touch a penny of the money that had been sent for the monument.

This same frame of mind is also reflected in his attitude toward the nomination of papal representatives to foreign countries. He would always exact a promise from such men before submitting their names for approval. The promise was that they would never accept money, gifts, or offerings of any kind, for any reason whatsoever, so that Catholics and non-Catholics alike could see in the Pope's representative a perfect example of absolute disinterest in the things of this world.

The Cardinal was in a position to make such a demand because he himself had an aversion to any sort of gift that might seem designed to limit his freedom of action. More than once he returned gifts, but in such a way as not to offend the donor. When for some special reason he could not refuse the gift, he would never attach any significance to it, or at times he would not even acknowledge it. Shortly before his death, a person who was trying to win his support had the bad taste to make him a gift of a case of different kinds of wines. The Cardinal was greatly displeased at a gesture so completely lacking in propriety. Since he did not want to mortify the donor by returning his gift he immediately sent off the case of wines to a poor religious community and the donor did not receive so much as a note of thanks.

The only things the Cardinal enjoyed receiving were little objects of piety and devotion, but they had to be plain and of slight value. The Superior of the Roman home of the Little Company of Mary had sent him a small marble statue

The Spiritual Life of Cardinal Merry del Val

of the Blessed Virgin that could well have been called a work of art. The Cardinal thanked the Mother Superior but delicately rebuked her at the same time, making it quite clear to her that she was not to send him anything of such value in the future.

There is still another aspect of his life that followed logically in the wake of his detachment from earthly possessions, and that was his modest way of living. This was especially evident from the house where he passed the last years of his life as Archpriest of St. Peter's—the insignificant Palazzina of Santa Marta hidden away in the shadow of the gigantic Vatican Basilica.

On the first floor were the rooms of the prince of the Church, but even they were kept within the limits of a dignified and serene austerity.

On the second floor were the rooms reserved for his private life.

Here, "where the spirit of his beloved St. Francis of Assisi seemed to hold sway," as Father Denis Sheil, the Cardinal's cousin said, there was no evidence of luxury or extravagance. There were merely a few plain pieces of furniture; just enough for his needs. His little bedroom looked like the cell of a monk. There was a little iron bed with a black finish and metal springs; on it there was a woolen mattress. It was the old bed he used as a student in Rome back in 1885 and on which he had slept for forty-five long years.

A "little hole in the wall" is the way the Cardinal used to refer to the room that he used for his study.

The only exception to this rule of utmost simplicity was to be found in his private chapel, which was richly adorned and really beautiful. The gold chalices and beautifully decorated altar reflected constant care and attention. The

In the Footsteps of the Saints

velvet curtains and vestments were of the most costly material, while the surplices and altar linens were always immaculate and of the finest and most delicately woven material.

For the Lord, all the magnificence and splendor that could go into his act of worship: truly a manifestation of his wonderful faith. For himself, nothing but utter simplicity and self-imposed poverty: this was a manifestation of his great humility.

For his own personal use he had nothing of any value; he did not have a single object made of gold. The watch he used ordinarily was a plain metal one with an indulgenced chain attached that is commonly known as that of "St. Peter's Chains." For his silver jubilee as a bishop, his beloved boys of Trastevere had intended to give him a gold watch. But he let them know in advance that he would not have accepted it, and besides he wanted to avoid putting them to an unnecessary expense. Instead, he accepted a silver watch which he always used from then on, just as twenty-five years earlier he had accepted from them an unpretentious pectoral cross as a remembrance of his consecration as Archbishop of Nicaea.

The buckles on his shoes were made of metal or simply silver-plated. He had only one pair of rich buckles and they were used only when he attended solemn ceremonies.

When at home he always wore a plain black cassock that gave no indication whatsoever of the high rank he held. He had only two pairs of house slippers and he wore the older pair practically all the time.

Nothing was more natural than that the servant of God should have practiced self-mortification to a point where he could apply to himself the words of the Apostle: "Always bearing about in our body the dying of Jesus, so that the life also of Jesus may be made manifest in our bodily frame" (2

The Spiritual Life of Cardinal Merry del Val

Cor. 4, 10). At the time he entered the Accademia dei Nobili Ecclesiastici there was a President who, certainly with the best possible intentions, provided the students with excessively frugal meals. Naturally, there were many complaints from the students and each one tried to provide himself with some food from outside the Academy. But that was not the case with the son of the Spanish Ambassador who, all the while he was a student there, never once allowed himself any food except what he got in the Academy.

That is the way he always was: extremely frugal. He never gave orders for food or indicated what he wanted: with utmost indifference he would eat what was put before him without ever manifesting a preference for this or that food and never commenting about the way in which it had been prepared. The members of his household attest that they never heard him remark that he liked or disliked a certain food, and no one ever knew exactly what his tastes were.

His cook one day made this observation: "I have been in his service for a long while and I can affirm that he never made even the slightest observation to me either about the quality of the food or about the way in which it was prepared. To him any kind of food was good and he would eat it without ever saying a word."

It is easily understood, therefore, why he never held parties or had many guests, and if he did on a special occasion invite a close relative or an intimate friend to his house, he never let it affect the customary frugality. We can readily understand, then, how Cardinal Canali could make the following statement: "His Eminence practiced self-mortification in everything he did. No one ever heard him express a desire for this or that, or complain because he did not have something or other. He never called the servants

In the Footsteps of the Saints

unless it was in a case of necessity. This was not only out of a sense of courtesy and refinement that was part of his nature, but primarily because of that spirit of mortification which he had learned to exercise over himself from the earliest years of his life."

The Cardinal's spirit of mortification was particularly edifying whenever he had some ailment. Monsignor Joseph Pescini, the Private Chaplain of St. Pius X, who both during and after the pontificate of this saintly Pope was in frequent contact with the servant of God, has left us this testimonial: "He was calm and serene at all times, and if questioned about some ailment that he was suffering he invariably replied with that wonderful smile of resignation, so characteristic of him, with which he was always able to conceal so many of his troubles and inner suffering, his many aches and pains."

It is no wonder, then, that his spirit of mortification in the last days of his life assumed the proportions and the splendor of extraordinary virtue.

Here is the testimony of the two Sisters, infirmarians of the Servants of Mary, who attended him in January, 1929, when he was stricken by an attack of influenza, and in February, 1930, in his last very brief illness. "We tended him in January of 1929 for a whole month and we can truthfully state that we always saw him in complete control of himself—something that is very difficult during a period of sickness. This was a definite manifestation and proof of his great virtue. He never asked for anything or refused anything. There was never a complaint, never a show of impatience. Only sometimes he would say: 'Do I have to take all of this?' and, when you told him 'yes,' then he would take it immediately even if it were something extremely distasteful. Everything that you did for him was,

The Spiritual Life of Cardinal Merry del Val

according to him, well done.

"One day we complained to him that he never let us know what he liked so that we might be better able to prepare things for him. The answer he gave us was:

'You do everything so well for me that I could not want anything better.' He was completely indifferent with respect to medicines and food and we got the impression that it did not matter at all to him what he ate.

"And now we come to February, 1930, and the end of his life. When the doctors declared that an operation was absolutely necessary, he lowered his eyes, bowed his head slightly as in submission to the will of God, then he said with full resignation: 'Go right ahead,' with never a change in his tranquillity of spirit, and as if nothing serious were happening.

"Many times we took his temperature but never once did he ask what his temperature was although he could not help but feel that it was very high. Although his mouth was burning up with fever, he never asked for water. Only once did he say: 'My mouth is very dry.

He practiced mortification to such a degree that we can state we never met another person who combined nobility and virtue in such a high degree. All that we saw in him served to edify us and was worthy of a perfect and saintly priest."

The Cardinal died when he was still in the full vigor of his manhood, and with his death there was brought to light a secret which had remained inviolate up to that moment. In the bottom drawer of his desk, among his personal objects, there were found two instruments of penance: a discipline or scourge equipped with little iron points that were almost worn out by long and constant use and showed traces of dried blood, and two hair shirts made of little iron hooks

In the Footsteps of the Saints

closely woven together.

These penitential objects indicate his unquenchable thirst for the suffering and renunciation that used to make him cry out: "Cut away here, O my Jesus; burn and destroy here all there is in me that is not Thine."

Epilogue

ON MAY 30, 1952, in a solemn session at the International Eucharistic Congress of Barcelona, the Spanish bishops addressed a petition to the Holy Father that first recalled the striking figure of the Cardinal Secretary of State of St. Pius X and then concluded: "His reputation for sanctity has grown steadily among the people, but especially among the clergy, who look upon him as a saintly priest, one who is worthy of being given the honors of our altars."

The Spanish hierarchy followed up this petition with another letter written on July 10th addressed to the Sacred Congregation of Rites in which the Rev. P. Giacomo Flores, Rector of the Pontifical Spanish College in Rome, was introduced as Postulator of the Cause of Beatification and Canonization of the Servant of God.

The only thing lacking now was to see this petition of the Spanish hierarchy fully realized, especially since testimonials to the Cardinal had been received from people all over the world.

The *Osservatore Romano* on February 27, 1953, published the news that the Ordinary Informative Process had been officially opened in the case of Cardinal Merry del Val with the following words:

The twenty-third anniversary of the pious death of Cardinal Merry del Val, today February 26th, marks a memorable date in the unending tribute of affection and veneration for the never-to-be-forgotten Cardinal.

This very morning, in one of the rooms on the first floor of the Vatican palace, with the consent of the Sovereign Pontiff, an ecclesiastical tribunal was officially constituted to begin the Ordinary Informative Process of investigating

The Spiritual Life of Cardinal Merry del Val

the sanctity, virtues, and miracles of the Servant of God, Cardinal Raphael Merry del Val, Secretary of State of Blessed Pius X.

The Cause of his Beatification thus takes the first important step toward realization.

As a fitting close to this book, we can cast a final glance at the saintly Pope who "restored all things in Christ" and at his faithful Secretary of State, recalling to mind that beautiful passage in Dante's *The Divine Comedy* where the poet celebrates the heavenly glory enjoyed by St. Francis of Assisi and his co-worker in Christ, St. Dominic:

"Where one is, the other worthily should also be; That as their warfare was alike, alike should be their glory" (Par. 12,34-36).

Other Titles you may like from Mediatrix Press

On the Marks of the Church
by St. Robert Bellarmine, S.J.

St. John Fisher: Reformer, Humanist, Martyr
E.E. Reynolds

The True Story of the Sword in the Stone:
A Compendium of the life of St. Galgano
Torchj Dei Galetti

St. Therese and the Faithful
by Benedict Williamson

The Life of St. Francis of Assisi
by Rev. Candide Chalippe, O.F.M.

The Franciscan Way of the Cross
Latin-English
Translated by Ryan Grant

A Champion of the Church: The life of St. Peter Canisius, S.J.
By William Reany, D.D.

A Small Catechism for Catholics by St. Peter Canisius
Translated by Ryan Grant
with a foreword by Fr. Chad Ripperger, PhD

As the Morning Star: The Life of St. Dominic
Rev. Jerome Wilms, O.P.

www.ingramcontent.com/pod-product-compliance
Lightning Source LLC
Chambersburg PA
CBHW032054090426
42744CB00005B/210